One-Way Tickets

One-Way Tickets

Writers and
the Culture of Exile

Alicia Borinsky

Trinity University Press
San Antonio

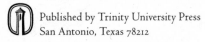 Published by Trinity University Press
San Antonio, Texas 78212

Jacket design by Anne Richmond Boston
Book design by BookMatters, Berkeley

Trinity University Press strives to produce its books using methods and
materials in an environmentally sensitive manner. We favor working with
manufacturers that practice sustainable management of all natural resources,
produce paper using recycled stock, and manage forests with the best
possible practices for people, biodiversity, and sustainability.

The press is a member of the Green Press Initiative, a nonprofit program
dedicated to supporting publishers in their efforts to reduce their impacts
on endangered forests, climate change, and forest dependent communities.

This book is printed on Rolland Enviro Natural, recycled from 100%
post-consumer waste.

The paper used in this publication meets the minimum requirements of
the American National Standard for Information Sciences—Permanence
of Paper for Printed Library Materials, ANSI Z39.48-1992.

Library of Congress Cataloging-in-Publication Data

Borinsky, Alicia.
One-way tickets : writers and the culture of exile / Alicia Borinsky.
    p.   cm.
Includes bibliographical references.
Summary: "Borinsky discusses the works of writers in exile, including
Vladimir Nabokov, writing in English in the United States, Julio Cortázar
in Paris, and Witold Gombrowicz in Buenos Aires, as well as Jorge Luis
Borges, Isaac Bashevis Singer, Oscar Hijuelos, Cristina Garcia, Junot Diaz,
and Clarice Lispector"—Provided by publisher.
ISBN 978-1-59534-070-2 (alk. paper)
1. Exiles' writings—History and criticism. 2. Authors, Exiled—20th
century. 3. Literature, Modern—20th century—History and criticism.
4. Expatriation in literature. 5. Alienation (Social psychology) in literature.
6. Immigration in literature. 7. Culture in literature. I. Title.

PN495.B67 2011
809'.899206914—dc22   2010044221

15   14   13   12   11   5   4   3   2   1

For Jeffrey, Natalia, Ezra, and Michal,
my here and there.

Contents

Acknowledgments

Friends, colleagues, and family have stimulated and supported me in ways both explicit and intangible in the making of the present volume.

I wrote early versions of the chapters on Isaac Bashevis Singer and Jean Rhys in response to invitations by Marc Shell and Susan Suleiman to contribute to volumes they each edited related to exile, and the piece on Reinaldo Arenas for a lecture organized by Norman Holland. I owe to Alberto Manguel and Edgardo Cozarinsky the discovery of Albert Londres, one the many gifts of their friendship and intelligence, and to Juan Mandelbaum many an insight about the presence of those who disappear.

Conversations with Sylvia Molloy, Sarli Mercado, Natalia Mehlman, Hugo Becaccece, Carlos Bruck, Julio Crespo, and Ivonne Bordelois have helped me refine my ideas of the impact that geographical displacement has on our languages. The technical savvy of Ezra Mehlman and Max Ubelaker Andrade, and their interest and dedication to the project, helped me resolve formatting issues in the early stages and provided me with intellectual stimulation. Steven Katz and Victoria Aarons encouraged me in the last stages of this book. I thank Barbara Ras and Sarah Nawrocki, as well as the team at Trinity University Press, for the care with which they executed every task.

Jeffrey Mehlman, my husband, is not only an implied interlocutor in these pages but also home, no matter where I may be.

A Samovar's Tale

My paternal grandmother arrived in Argentina from Russia with her husband and five children in 1919. As a child, when my family gathered at her apartment, I listened, rapt, to my older cousins speak in hushed tones about the big secret— her marriage as a young girl to her older uncle, with the resulting double last name Borinsky de Borinsky. Whispers, as though her own life were too transgressive for my grandmother to hear about.

That first husband, our grandfather, had died before we were born. To me, he was a Russian in the same unbelievable dimension as Rasputin or Stalin, a ghost of the old country, unable to speak Spanish, inscrutable. Whenever I visited my grandmother, I glimpsed him, tall and dressed in black, in the imposing wedding picture on the wall above her bed, with my grandmother, a mere adolescent in an elaborate lace wedding dress beside him. Yet although I found this portrait fascinating, another artifact was even more compelling to my imagination: a glistening silver samovar.

The samovar sat in the living room atop an oversized mahogany sideboard. Indeed, all the furniture in the modest apartment was too big, bought, perhaps, with the dimensions of my grandparents' Russian home in mind. I saw it as a testimony to their having been somehow shipwrecked in the city of my birth. The samovar, brought from so far away, had a prestige that I, born in a chance location imposed by history, knew I lacked. Sitting in that living room, listening to the stories of my grandparents' flight, as Jews who spoke Russian, not Yiddish, and proudly declared themselves among the wealthy minority, who heroically conquered dangers in the woods until finally they boarded the legendary boat that brought them to Buenos Aires, I'd think about the samovar and the experiences it embodied.

When I was a child I imagined parties in fairy tale castles, and my grandmother as a young girl surrounded by toys. Then came the nightmarish scenario of her being snatched away by a bandit who looked exactly like her first husband.

Gradually, I came to see the samovar as a symbol of past wealth, an abstraction that differentiated my father's family from the rest of immigrant Jews, who were perhaps too poor or, the opposite, too rich and materialistic. The claim of uniqueness through an aristocratic past was, of course, not uncommon, fueled by anxiety over being confused for what they actually were: eager, needy immigrants. At the same time, it all became part of the intimation of the sexuality of another age, of life in closed communities, crisscrossed by family ties in which wives and husbands, though occupying different spaces, might well be related by blood. I felt that Jewish shtetls were simultaneously foreign and familiar, and that the landing of my family in Argentina almost was a change of planet.

How do you flee running through the woods toting young children and a samovar? How do you bring with you the *iberbeds*, those oversized down comforters that would be handed down to each of the five children at the time of their marriage?

My father was just two years old when he arrived in Buenos Aires. My experience was of a man who spoke only Spanish, loved movies, taught me how to dance tango, and had nothing but jokes about his legacy, imitating Jewish accents and gestures as he parodied that life he never knew. And yet, three times a week after work he was drawn to his mother's apartment before he came back home to us for dinner. He went for the tea poured from the samovar, the homemade jellies, Russian stories. These visits were a source of tension between my parents. But to my mother's putdowns of backward Russians, my father responded only with silence, an eloquent shrug.

Perhaps they did not need to flee. Perhaps they had time to prepare for the trip and carefully packed the samovar, sheets, tablecloths, and silverware, everything we saw in my grandmother's apartment. Or perhaps they did flee and acquired those objects later in Argentina. Who knows? No matter how much my grandmother talked about arriving in Argentina, I knew that it was just a tale. I understood the message of the samovar. It stood silently on the sideboard warning me not to trust her.

Exile, I learned very early on, was about telling a story. The bewilderment of being elsewhere, the enduring incredulity at having left, and the celebration of the new place all needed some heroic originating act. One could not simply *show up* in the new country. There had to be a why, a when, and a how of getting there. Those were the questions that had to be answered. Not merely who your parents were, the places of your childhood. The answers had clear implications: *I know that I do not belong in this place; if I tell you how it happened, you will understand and acknowledge my right to be among you.*

My maternal grandfather arrived in Argentina from Poland on his own in 1934 and worked in a furniture factory to earn enough money to send for his wife and children. My mother was the last one to make it out of Poland, in 1936; her mother and one sister were not so lucky, and I grew up hearing their names in special service broadcasts of the Red Cross designed to locate possible survivors. I learned only recently that all the Jews of their town, Slonim, perished.

My grandfather did not bring a samovar; he talked about socialism, against religion, and was a universalist who believed that he had landed in a savage country. He endured Peronism and military coups with the irony of one who knows where the world is heading. Contemptuous of the literal interpretations of the tradition and what he termed superstitions of orthodox Jews he told instead stories of Jewish secular heroes: the musicians, philosophers, artists, and scientists who justified his own existence. He convinced me as a child that Spinoza, Marx, Freud, Trotsky, Kafka, and Einstein were my own passport to understanding how things worked. His way of being a person, of overcoming the humiliating massacre of European Jewry, was to flaunt this extraordinary baggage. Though a woodcarver in a furniture store, he believed himself a true artist and revolutionary as he continued to mount his adolescent rebellion against his father, a rabbi. And I was to be his helper, as a writer and a polyglot philologist. After all, from among his grandchildren he had picked me to write his biography, and presuming that someday I would have to escape from political persecution in Argentina, I would have to learn languages for my own safety.

His stories had the suspense of a cliffhanger, always reaching a climax when, at being questioned by a German, Pole, or Russian, he would respond in a flawless accent, thereby passing as one of them and avoiding violence. He related his stories to me in Yiddish but reproduced the dialogue in the various original languages spoken by the participants in the events. I could sense the menace of interlocutors, the closeness of danger. Great drama. Great theater. I was not blind, though, and I also could see that my grandfather, with his big ears and nose, looked unmistakably like the Jew he was trying to save by feats of pronunciation and grammar. But I also knew he was right in his admonishment: *You see? That's why you've got to study and learn; there's nothing like languages to save your life, open your mind, speed you away from persecution.*

The time came when, following a military takeover in Argentina, I did have to leave. His self-aggrandizing stories then became uncannily pertinent. Speaking several languages has made me more versatile, and although I am not working on his biography, I am still trying to tease meaning out of his life as a writer.

As far as my cousins and I could tell, our Russian grandmother never left her apartment whereas my Polish grandfather would go for frequent walks to destinations he liked to keep secret. Whatever they did each day, their experiences outside the circle of close relatives were not part of our conversation. And although they never said so outright, it was clear that both of them were bewildered at having arrived in Buenos Aires with changed names and a new language.

For both sides of my family, the difficult voyage to Argentina was their roots. Nobody spoke of Russian pogroms or the vast Jewish graveyard of Poland, though those were the experiences of their youth. Admittedly, recollections of foods, people, and places would sometimes overcome them, but they quickly brushed them aside, the way one muffles a sneeze or closes a window to prevent a draft.

People who had been on the same boat became *shifshvesters* and *shifbruders*, an extended family I came to regard as my own aunts, uncles, and cousins. Some of them had numbers tattooed on their forearms, evident in the summer, on the beach, shiny under tanning oil. They were not exiles but immigrants. They held one-way tickets and developed a nervous allegiance to a country that gave shelter not only to them but also to their enemies, the war criminals who arrived aided by Perón's government.

My family is not unusual in Argentina. For my parents and their brothers and sisters, Eastern Europeans with varying degrees of hostility toward countries that spat them out and massacred those who stayed on, Buenos Aires remained foreign and suspect. Despite enjoying the city's cosmopolitan cultural offerings of good food and high fashion, they also acknowledged its brutal tendency toward anti-Semitism with a fatalism born of the circumstances that had landed them there.

We, children of these immigrants, in contrast, were born into a secular, integrated society in constant financial crisis. The overall feeling for this younger generation was that of belonging. We did not regard ourselves as stranded like our forebears or like the numerous Spanish Republicans who year in, year out waited patiently for news of Franco's death so that they might return to Spain.

It was only when I left Argentina to escape its bloody dictatorships that I experienced for myself the longing that in the past had seemed so quaint in others. I now know what it means to pack one's bags not for a short stay, but for good, selecting what one will retain of a home that is no longer a shelter but a threat. My indispensable items were in their way perhaps equivalent to the things my Russian grandmother and Polish grandfather brought with them to Argentina: books I could not do without, musical recordings I feared I would be unable to find elsewhere, shoes to weather a climate I had never encountered. As I shared my stories and personal experiences, sitting in apartments in Europe and the United States, with people close to my age, the seesawing emotions toward Argentina that I had witnessed in the immigrants around me became my own.

The long lines at the Italian and Spanish embassies in Buenos Aires after the 2001 collapse of the Argentine economy, made up of the children and grandchildren of immigrants trying to escape economic strife by claiming the right to European nationality, are a commentary on the complexity of the allegiance that the country inspires.

Jorge Luis Borges, the great questioner of geographical and historical certainties, is said to have commented that rather than citizens, Argentina has inhabitants—or better yet, several million people all clamoring for room service at once. Whether he actually said this or not, the observation catches the peculiar nature of a country defined by the idea of travel, with real life as something to be experienced elsewhere. Although immigrants assimilated, working hard and investing emotionally in their adopted country, an air of self-doubt prevailed among my compatriots. Native Argentines looked to Europe for true culture, and transplanted Europeans, while praising the wealth of natural resources now at their disposal, hoped one day to experience again the real thing.

That first departure was for me unlike any other, and even if I now return frequently to an Argentina with a much altered political and social atmosphere, the distance traveled on that first trip remains immeasurably vast.

The word *trip* falls far short of describing my experience of leaving. Before my departure, I developed an urgent need to locate all of my personal manuscripts and the translations into Spanish I had done of my favorite English and American poets. Yet even once I'd gathered them all together, I realized that I still had to make choices, since there was not enough room in my suitcases for everything. It all resulted in a feeling of loss, accompanied by a sense that, light as I had become, I could go anywhere. This was no trip; it was a change in the very rhythm of my experiences, an exiting from the world of shared memory.

Once I'd arrived abroad, I developed an anxiety about the efficiency of the post office since this was before the era of electronic mail. In the early seventies the Chilean writer José Donoso, admonishing me to write letters more frequently, declared that the post office is a writer's true homeland, and once I had left Argentina his words rang truer than ever. Now that regular address changes, long-distance friendships, and the weave of foreignness and familiarity have become part of the way I see the world, my notion of a true homeland encompasses that area that Cortázar calls "la zona," the shared, familiar in-betweenness of many trips.

My anxiety about the post office was somewhat misplaced because I am not a good letter writer. My letters are few and far between, fueled usually either by a momentary enthusiasm or an acute feeling of guilt. The messages I send tend to be oblique, due perhaps to my awareness that they can never take the place of a close hug or a shared cup of coffee.

I have a long-standing fascination with writers and artists who are known in part for their peculiar displacement. A brief list includes, in Paris: Walter Benjamin, exploring his Jewishness in a city he made his own through a fragmented stroll of its arcades; Julio Cortázar, whose uncannily upbeat grave in the Montparnasse cemetery—featuring a statue by Julio Silva, a triumph of an Argentine friendship built in Paris—stands as a de facto resolution to the conflict enunciated in the two part-titles of his novel *Hopscotch,* "Del lado de aquí" (From here) and "Del lado de allá" (From there);[1] and Jean Rhys, itinerant inhabitant of Left Bank hotels that helped her weave the character of the uprooted woman as an aimless poseur and outsider. Buenos Aires, London, towns and cities in the United States and Brazil, became permanently temporary homes to writers such as Vladimir Nabokov, Isaac Bashevis Singer, Witold Gombrowicz, and Clarice Lispector, all of whom provide us with a textured and multivariate sense of distance that exists outside of maps.

This book speaks about foreigners who do not take shelter in nostalgia, ethnic affirmation, and group identity, but who explore the puzzle of cultural transitions through their own experience, as new languages, customs, tastes, sounds, and smells intervene to transform acquired tastes and expectations. It considers the fundamental expression of substance, color, and density of an individual life, and the defining moment when somebody becomes distinguishable from all others.

I have also tried to answer what for me is an unavoidable question: Where and what is my samovar? It is probably embedded somewhere in tango lyrics and in the itineraries that make up the imaginary city of my fiction and poetry. Writing in the United States in English and Spanish, I am a Latina. Publishing in Argentina in Spanish, I am an Argentine living abroad. Everywhere I am a woman. Everywhere Jewish. No longer an exiled student, I am now a mobile writer. As I write these pages in English in Boston, I move in and out of familiar sounds within a conversation not too far, in its relationship to my native language, from those I heard in Spanish in Argentina during my childhood.

How, in this time of instant communication and easy transportation, is one to understand that there are irreversible trips? How do we superimpose the reality of irretrievable time on the predictability of the round-trip ticket? And what about those for whom a round trip would be a nightmare, who are fleeing something they never want to experience again? Once they leave by boat, raft, plane, train, bus, car, or horse, or walk across a border alone or in a group, everything changes.

We would rather refuse the seduction of the samovar in telling our own lives because our hope is to find and speak the truth, without nostalgic embellishments, even though we know that the nature of storytelling itself conspires against such austerity—which is why I shall probably never write a straightforward autobiography. The reflections I offer in this book turn around books, music, films, and television programs that in speaking intimately to me have helped me understand the shape and tone of my own story.

The nineteenth-century novel, whose absence is bemoaned by many, lives on in film, popular television shows, and the literature of travel, self-help, and autobiography. The idea of a character at the center of historical and social events, a person around whom everything revolves and for whom details fall meaningfully into place, still commands our imagination. It suggests coherence, arranges life as a sequence of actions and consequences.

Exiles, immigrants, expatriates, and refugees have frequently organized their experiences to fight their lack of a familiar context. They are either invisible, as in the works of Nina Berberova, or they stand out, as does Pnin in Nabokov's novel or Jean Rhys's women in Paris. Blending in is a goal for some, an impossibility for others. Personal accounts or fictional narratives with that kind of situation in mind are reminiscent of the nineteenth-century novel: they give us a person at the center of the story, a protagonist, man or woman, as the measure of all things.

Current interest in biographies and autobiographies reflects our effort to ward off the hollowness of contemporary life. We go to the movies, we scan bookstore shelves, and come into contact with people who have lived their lives with purpose, sometimes playing a decisive social or historical role, aware of them for their heroism or because they are at the heart of a scandal.

In these pages cultural snapshots are signposts for our experience. Each section presents exiles, both real and fictional. Whether these accounts are factual or invented does not matter; the logic of the samovar blurs specific differences, while giving a glimpse of something else, slightly askew, separating newcomers from those around them.

Newcomers need translation. Life is presented again to

them (to us) as a de-naturalized exercise, something up for grabs and always risking misunderstanding.

When we arrive in a city for the first time, having left the familiar behind, possibly for good, we benefit from its energy and partake of the possibility of reinventing ourselves. We think here beyond the suntan, the souvenirs, and the museum visits of tourism, so often summarized in mere terms of cultural enrichment, photographs to share with friends back home, a few foreign words that immediately lose their meaning. Living in a new city calls on us to be in a heightened state of alertness. The anonymity of persons in the street, the overlapping of their stories, the fragmented nature of overheard conversations renders an instant sense of theater, a detachment that comes from being unable to understand everything offered to us as we blend into a mass of strangers with faces and customs of their own.

The freedom some of us feel in urban spaces, whether at home or abroad, may very well be illusory, given the present ubiquity of virtual images and the homogeneity of worldwide fashion. The Gap T-shirt worn with a peasant skirt by an Indian woman eating pizza in Buenos Aires strikes us as both dissonant and meaningful.

Is this freedom? Are today's cities with their invitations to consumerism what we need to foster the kind of collage we may have become?

This book takes us to Buenos Aires, New York, Paris, sites in Poland and Russia. These are places to which I am intimately linked, and yet illusions of self-discovery have startled me more than once as I have revisited them through the lives and works I explore here. How separate are books, films, and art from what we call real experience? Rather than answering the question directly, I have elicited from the gallery of characters and experiences in this book the manner in which differences become blurred. At times, I evoke authors' lives as they intersect with their works; at others, the autobiographical gives shape, as though I were part of the tale. I have opted for the equivalent of simultaneous translation: each seemingly unique life illuminates another, giving both new meaning.

At the same time, I have tried to configure a kind of photo album in which memory, displacement, contempt, false pride, and self-delusion are all at play. We glimpse cultures clashing and being stifled in the United States, Europe, and Argentina, as the relative and frequently forged uniqueness of ethnic groups is redefined.

I try to bring out inflections, gestures, and poses: the frictions and judgments conveyed by sideway glances and stares directed at or by people defined variously as visitors, intruders, guests, or citizens. These come from books, movies, television shows, and tango lyrics, with high undifferentiated from low, for our experience of estrangement and belonging is intricately woven into every level of culture.

Similarly, the stories assembled here are at once exemplary and idiosyncratic. Often, exiles and immigrants represent themselves as swimming against the flow of a society that increasingly blends differences, even as it seems to celebrate them through the ideology of multiculturalism.

Many students of culture, in their search for what it means to be Cuban, Puerto Rican, Asian, or anything else, respond by lauding these individuals as epic characters, while at the same time cloaking them in assumed ethnic attributes, ways of communication, and political allegiances, thereby rendering them invisible. The struggles with language and self-presentation in the works of Oscar Hijuelos and Isaac Bashevis Singer, the conflicts between worlds new and old in Reinaldo Arenas and Vladimir Nabokov, and the attention to dress, manner, and vocabulary in Jean Rhys and Manuel Puig all speak to a sensibility stemming from the tension between the local and the universal, the omnipresence of cultural differences, and the frequent mirages that fictionalize their resolution.

A different danger resides in stories of individuals who become nourished by fictions of singularity and succumb to the perceived prestige of the marginal. Jorge Luis Borges, Julio Cortázar, Alejandra Pizarnik, and Clarice Lispector may be seen as belonging in this register.

By taking the perspective of an exile, of someone who is not at home with any clear-cut definition or univocal perspective but would rather subject herself to the surprises of simultaneous translation, I hope to have avoided either of these traps. The literary snapshots assembled here reveal how going from there to here, being uprooted and either finding or forever missing a place to claim as one's own, is a mark of contemporary culture. I have not attempted to explain away the puzzlement that so many feel at needing to reinvent themselves in a foreign country. Nor, because exilic perspective is about discontinuity, have I attempted to create a linear narrative. This book embraces the contagion of the nomadic, the unclassifiable, the foreign. Each chapter turns into a different aspect of why and how somebody gets encrypted somewhere.

In spite of tenacious differences, others will join me, I hope in finding aspects of their own trips in these pages, whether they really took off or just dream of a one-way ticket untamed by the round-trip reassurances of tourism and organized travel.

Stranded

The city, its mirages

The architecture of Buenos Aires intrigues some and exasperates others with its mixed styles reminiscent of cities left behind. The French writer and adventurer Antoine de Saint-Exupéry, who visited Buenos Aires in 1929, was thoroughly put off by its look and by the francophilia that he detected among the *porteños* he met. His biographer Stacy Schiff reports his view of Buenos Aires: "Every well-bred Argentine thought himself spiritually and culturally a Frenchman, but all her love of France could not make Buenos Aires look like Paris. A house dating from 1890 was considered old; the city's architecture was a jumble of steel and concrete New York–style skyscrapers, French-inspired *hôtels particuliers,* and small colonial homes, all piled atop one another."[1] Clearly, Saint-Exupéry did not find that Buenos Aires had enough character to justify the time and peril of getting there. It was all too French, or too would-be French.

Something else must have been playing as well in Saint-

Exupéry's imagination; that something, to quote Borges, was no doubt "that Argentine passion, snobbery." Even more, Saint-Exupéry's displeasure likely stemmed from seeing nothing that was typically *porteño* in Buenos Aires. But what would that be? Buenos Aires often feels like a mirage, since so many spots could be confused with Madrid, Palermo, Paris, London. Buenos Aires architecture is made up of quotations; its itineraries eloquently show the arrivals of different groups with their mixed hopes for belonging and departure, creating a triumphant argument for decontextualization.

The look of Buenos Aires, though distinct, is borrowed. It stems from the city's enduring myth, tango, a promise of exile enmeshed in the experience of love. You cannot say that you have actually experienced Buenos Aires if you do not have some understanding of tango, with its implied choreography of encounters, disappointments, and passions. That was what was missing from Saint-Exupéry's experience, which made him blind to the character of a city that pulsated beyond buildings.

The very landscape of Buenos Aires suggests a kind of daydreaming projected by the scattered stylistic allegiances for other places expressed in its architecture. People sitting in cafés and bars and milling about in the street are seen by tango as forever waiting for someone or recovering from someone having left. Buenos Aires is a city of departures and yet it has the capacity to seduce, to make itself be missed; the very skepticism of its roots becomes a unique source of recognition.

Tango is a register for interpretation, a map that decodes the poses of characters in bars, praises certain street corners and neighborhoods, warns of the dangers of downtown glitter, and laments the fate of those banned from honest destinies behind the doors of one-story houses in more humble areas of the city. At the same time, it creates the illusion that life is not lived in vain, because its tales give meaning to resentment and favor mistrust of the wealthy, the collective, and love. Women who come from afar, leave suddenly, or fade away are tango's way of naming one of its enduring beliefs.

Where did she go?

One classic story of how a man falls for a woman is told in the celebrated tango "Malevaje": "Te ví pasar tangueando altanera / con un compás tan hondo y sensual / que no fue más que verte y perder / la fe, el coraje y el ansia 'e luchar" (I saw you pass me by in a tango step / so haughty / so deep / so sensual / that as soon as I saw you / I lost the faith, courage, urge to fight). The male voice is addressing a woman who has mesmerized him. Her sensuality has transformed him: once a swaggering rabble rouser, he started attending mass and abandoned his friends, losing his old way of life. The woman's magnetism defeats his male posturing and turns him into a lovesick suitor, in a fall from grace. For "Malevaje," manhood is distinct from love. Being a man means staying with the boys in the rough knife-wielding neighborhoods where only violence wins respect. Yet this woman has managed to turn him inside out. Her body, perfectly attuned to the cadences of tango, promises a path of pleasure, but exclusively for two. No male friends; no visits to mother.

Tango teaches that a seductress, sinuous and entrancing but never quite honest, is always capable of destroying the paradoxical harmony of the violent male world. A man's success in conquering such a woman is synonymous with the deterioration of his life. In this sense, tango is deeply suspicious of love, or as it so frequently turns out to be, maddening infatuation. "La ingrata," the ungrateful, undeserving woman, may be a prostitute or adulteress, or she may stay for a while then disappear from her lover's life, leaving him in debt and ridiculed by the friends he left behind, who warned him of the dangers awaiting him. The lyrics of another classic, "Aquel tapado de armiño" (That ermine coat), tell of the jilted lover with such eloquence as to have kept the composition in tango repertories for decades: "Aquel tapado de armiño / todo forrado en lamé / que tu cuerpito abrigaba / al salir del cabaret. / Cuando pasate a mi lado, / prendida a aquel gigoló / aquel tapado de armiño. / ¡Cuánta pena me causó!"

As the man sees his lover leaving the nightclub on a gigolo's arm, wearing an ermine coat that he is still paying for, the cost of the coat becomes the measure of his mistake. Now her victim, he recalls the sacrifices he made to buy the coat, even as she dons it for a life that ruins his hopes for the future. The woman in the ermine coat is no lady; she has left him to go out cavorting with sleazy nightclub characters. If the woman in "Malevaje," viewed with admiring glances as she sashays by on the dance floor, promises an intensity of pleasure that she then betrays by turning her man into a domesticated suitor, the sin of the woman in "Aquel tapado de armiño" is the opposite: she goes from being a humble woman to a *milonguera*, a desirable woman fond of the nightlife in the tango bars, who turns on her sex appeal after she gets the coveted coat.[2]

It is not only on the dance floor but also in the streets of the city that the failures of love are inscribed and the mirages of infatuation forged, that glances, seductions, grievances, and betrayals are played out. Whether observing or being observed, the ones telling their story are at the same time telling the story of their the city. Their love is intertwined with their milieu, and walking becomes a rehearsal of false starts and intermittent successes. When they leave or are left, these characters are thrown back onto the streets, their paths now marked by a certain wisdom.

Tango does speak of good women, ones deserving of love and loyalty. Mothers and sick sisters tend to be above reproach. One of the best-known compositions sang by Carlos Gardel, arguably the most celebrated singer in tango history, is entitled "Victoria" and features a man who sings his joy (voicing victory) upon being left by his wife, for he will now be able to see his old friends again and go back to living with his mother ("volver a ver mis amigos / vivir con mama otra vez"). On the whole, though, such loyalty is found only after love has been defeated, and longing continues on, circling around the pain of loneliness.

The preferred locale for the telling of such a story is a table in a bar or café. The lyricist Pascual Contursi wrote the most representative of these compositions, "Mi noche triste" (My sad night): "Percanta que me amuraste / en lo mejor de mi vida, / dejándome el alma herida / y espinas en el corazón, / sabiendo que te quería / que vos eras mi alegría / y mi sueño abrasador, / para mí ya no hay consuelo / y por eso me encurdelo / pa' olvidarme de tu amor" (Nasty deceitful broad / you left me / in the flower of my life / wounded soul, thorns in my heart / knowing I wanted you / that you were my light and my most passionate dream / no consolation for me now / that's why I get drunk / hoping to forget your love).

The departure of the "good" woman redefines the space in which the romance took place; longing for her is one with bemoaning the loss of cozy domesticity and the gloominess of his surroundings now that she is gone. The serene harmony of the everyday, rather than anxiety provoked by the *milonguera*, is the mark of the worthwhile woman— who, however, is inevitably bound to disappoint. While the departure of an object of infatuation is a relief, associated though it may be with moral and financial ruin, the loss of a good woman dampens every aspect of daily life. And so the singer, when he goes to sleep at night, leaves the door open so that she may come back in, and he still brings home the little pastries she used to enjoy, while the bed, he claims, is angry because they are not both there: "De noche cuando me acuesto, / no puedo cerrar la puerta, / porque dejándola abierta / me hago ilusión que volvés. / Siempre llevo bizcochitos / pa' tomar con matecitos / como si estuvieras vos, / y si vieras la catrera / cómo se pone cabrera / cuando no nos ve a los dos."

The wealthy are regularly denounced by tango's populist lyrics. Men and women who dress up in fancy clothes and show off their money and jewels in night clubs, the *niños bien* and *pitucas* who abound in the city, are shown to be fakes at best, parasites at worst. The worthy woman of tango, in contrast, is humble in appearance, her qualities distinct from the nocturnal glitter and sexual intensity of pimps and prostitutes. Missing the woman thus also betrays nostalgia for an uncomplicated relationship to reality, one in which money does not play a decisive role.

In tango, appearance helps define the moral profiles of characters, creating a complicity with the listener who shares the singer's judgments. Thus, the shabby brown coat and hat of the departing María in the composition of that name are emblems of her kindness: "Acaso te llamaras solamente María, / no sé si eras el eco de una vieja canción, / pero hace mucho, mucho fuiste hondamente mía / sobre un paisaje triste, desmayado de amor. / El otoño te trajo, mojando de agonía, / tu sombrerito pobre y el tapado marrón. / Eras como la calle de la melancolía / que llovía . . . llovía sobre mi corazón." Perhaps, the singer tells the woman, her name was simply María; she might have been the echo of an old song, but he knows that a long, long time ago she was deeply his. The landscape was sad, rainy; brought in by autumn, María, with her humble clothes, was like the melancholy street raining on the singer's heart. In this manner, a humble young woman, now gone, is woven into the landscape with the certainty of goodness lost, her aura of moral uplift a result of her attire and the wound she has left forever associated with autumn and the streets in which she first appeared.

Humble women and humble neighborhoods convey the ethical conviction of tango, providing a momentary escape from the betrayals of glitz. It is on those subjects that tango lyrics lose their sharp-edged sarcasm and skepticism, wishing instead for the return of that harmonious state in which love, goodness, and simple pleasures coexist.

Time, however, erases the beauty of youth, thereby validating the misleading nature of all love. As the ubiquitous lament goes, "Y pensar que hace diez años fue mi locura / que llegué hasta la traición por tu hermosura / que esto que hoy es un cascajo fue la triste metedura / donde yo perdí el honor" (And to think that ten years ago I was so crazy about her / that I went as far as betrayal for her beauty / and that which is today an empty shell / was the sad infatuation / for which I threw away my honor). The opposite applies as well, as in Pascual Contursi's "Flor de fango" (Gutter flower), which tells the story, in *lunfardo*, of a beautiful girl who at age fourteen succumbs to "las delicias de un gotán" (the indulgences of tango) and leaves her simple but worthy home for the ongoing party. She, like so many women in tango tradition, has been coaxed into believing in love, only to be left alone, old and disillusioned. Tango punishes everybody: men and women are met with old age and decay, and the man suffers the added burden of the loss of his lover's beauty.

In tango, true distances are measured in terms of time, not space. Something decisive and morally abject resides in the pleasures of the night. Faking one's origins, dressing up, drinking and dancing, and enjoying fast money are each simultaneously the source and the obstacle to happiness in its lyrics.

She looks so special; where is she from?

The emergence of an urban reality in the first part of the twentieth century brought with it a new mobility for women. They are now increasingly represented on the go: working in offices and factories, selling groceries and knickknacks in markets, tending patients in hospitals, performing in vaudeville shows, circuses, and bars. These women, rather than evoking domesticity and motherhood, are unattached. A story is all the more powerful if it develops the drama of life outside the family. And the glitzier the women, the more attractive and feminine they become. The famous Ziegfeld Follies of the 1930s, with its assemblages of feathered, smiling chorus girls, not only suggested the gaiety of nightlife but also served as a register for the spaces emerging in the city.

The great female stars of Hollywood's golden age had an aura of remoteness that set them apart from everyday domesticity. Women with mysterious big eyes and distant expressions suggestive of tantalizing pasts beckoned one to imagine exciting possibilities.

Greta Garbo did not expect to gain success in the United States; as she wrote in a letter in 1926, "They don't have a type like me out here, so if I can't learn how to act, they'll soon tire of me." How wrong she was. The romance of distance was becoming alive in Hollywood, and her other-worldliness made her desirable beyond any specific role. Garbo was notorious for taking walks on the beach in Santa Monica, dressed in the trench coat and floppy hat that would become her signature. She did not want to be photographed smiling; her moody appearance of concentrating on an idea that was beyond the public's grasp was part of her aura.

If a certain apathy, an unwillingness to engage those around, was key to Garbo's magnetism, elegance, and intensity, the opposite, an illusion of direct contact, became a factor in Dolores del Río's fame, even before she had an important picture to her credit. Born in Mexico, she had big eyes and a penetrating gaze that were ideal for silent movies. In 1926, she was honored by the Western Association of Motion Picture Advertisers as a "baby star." Two years later she had achieved full-fledged star status for the silent films *What Price Glory?*, *Resurrection*, and *Ramona*.

Dolores del Río was portrayed as a partygoer, with her long evening dresses, matching fur stoles, and expensive jewelry. She enhanced her self-presentation by mixing Mexican ethnic styles, ruffles, bracelets, and geometric designs and prints with Parisian touches. The public found Dolores del Río's style, a glittering presence that suggested love and drama, fascinating, and it became an integral part of her persona.

And then there was Marlene Dietrich, whose life exceeded the roles she played in films. Extremely conscious of her appearance and the power of photography, she cross-dressed, as in the famous tuxedo shot, or wore ultrafeminine clothes that accentuated her slim body and long legs. When she came to Hollywood in 1930, she was thought of as competition for Garbo, but she soon took her career on a different path. Garbo and Dietrich, with their exotic accents, stilted presences, and air of androgyny, introduced the romance of distance and daring into their images. In real life, they transgressed sexual bounds as well, Dietrich with her bisexuality, Garbo by participating in the Hollywood lesbian scene. In a *Vanity Fair* photo spread that featured the pair, they were dubbed "Members of the Same Club."[3] Dietrich took freedom, insolence, arrogance, and courage a step farther when she sided against her native Germany during the war, actively opposing Nazism.

Claudette Colbert had a lighter touch. Born in France and raised in New York from the age of seven, she bore the imprint of her French upbringing. A friend said of her, "Claudette was more French than the French; she ran a French house, served only French food, and she had the natural clothes sense so typical of a French woman."[4] Colbert's style was muted and tailored, as she remained faithful to an image of France she had been fed from afar. The results had the precision and neatness of a fabrication.

Colbert worked both in films and on Broadway and managed to have a long career almost without changing her looks, unlike Joan Crawford, who transformed herself over the years with amazing success. Colbert's appeal was more understated than anybody else's because it had to do with her interpretation of a French natural style. It is widely known that she was prone to taking apart one of the seemingly simple suits that she frequently wore if she did not like a button or a detail in the lining. Colbert's image was not about sex but about briskness and access to the daily look of a hypothetical and minimalist Paris.

These actresses personified the idea of the immigrant or, in the case of Dietrich, the exile as a source of fascination and glamour. They used their foreignness to lure American imaginations out of ordinariness into a world open to the possibilities of fiction and the uncertainties of distance. *I am my own story,* said their faces in photos and on the screen. American-born actors and actresses, too, cultivated a sense of otherness by developing a special look, like Joan Crawford and Ava Gardner. And directors capitalized on their appeal by starring them in double roles as both actresses and personalities.

The goal was not to be naturalized into the everyday. Glamour shots of celebrities stepping out of limousines into crowds of fans were part of the show; they moved the public to imagine a less mundane, more exciting life. Buying a ticket to the movies meant going on a trip afforded by the stars.

Today, the sensibility is different: a feeling of proximity

and familiarity rather than remoteness and foreignness is the goal. Clothes are now a mainstream identity card, and the look is not to have a special look. Celebrities are photographed in shorts and running shoes more often than in evening wear. Even the outrageous attires of some popular music idols are designed to be replicated and worn by others. Television has brought home what used to be a special experience, and in so doing it has redefined our relationship to the screen. The public that watches reality shows is not interested in aloof glamour. Julia Roberts, the pretty woman, could be anybody when not in a movie—or so promises her pose. It is as though as travel became easier, distance ceased to have appeal. The great female stars of the past affected a pose that was removed from the everyday. They would have certainly been out of place in a den or a living room once television, the great normalizer, taught us how to stay home, body and mind.

Never go back:
Eva Perón and leaving one's class behind

Besides filling screens and magazines, the faces of Hollywood provided inspiration for newspaper coverage of political figures. Growing up in Argentina, I witnessed, even before I went to school, how the enduring myth of Eva Perón was being forged through staged photo opportunities.[5] She combined glamour and publicity to pioneer the kind of self-styling so prevalent today as politics merges with popular culture to shape public opinion.

Eva came to Buenos Aires from a small provincial town at the age of fifteen determined to make it in the big city. She immediately went about reinventing herself: she took lessons on how to speak properly, began articulating sounds in a different way, and had a change of appearance. Hers was a triumphant makeover that took place in front of the entire country, and there was the added promise that anybody could undertake the same voyage, breaking away from oppressive origins to enjoy the plentiful resources of a new, more equitable order.

Eva's opponents among the traditional upper classes of Argentina responded to her with the same contempt they had for tango. She *was* the fallen woman of tango: rather than staying poor and industrious, she made herself up, dressed in clothes she should have never been able to afford, and flaunted herself in the media. For them, Eva's cult was an insolent expression of the lower classes, vulgar and immoral. Her partisans—*su pueblo, sus descamisados*—in contrast, saw her as a saint and thanked her for the charm she showered on them through her deeds and personal appearances. They revered her for escaping poverty and turning her resentments into a powerful weapon, in a social transformation that changed Argentina forever. The glamour of Hollywood and the sinful glitter of tango came together in Eva's pose with an intensity that endured for years after her death.

Peronists saw themselves as representing the "true Argentina" against the snobbery and elitism of the upper classes. Their enemies, however, pointed to their links with fascist ideology and Nazism—which, among other things, allowed for a good number of war criminals to find shelter in Argentina with government support. In 1945, leftist and conservatives formed a coalition against Perón under the name La Unión Democrática. They were roundly defeated, however, in a campaign that spoke of the downtrodden, the new Argentina, and its national roots.

The mirages of national identity were fully in place: those who thought of themselves as universalist antifascists were portrayed as enemies of patriotic Argentines. Eva, poor and born out of wedlock in a lost town, an internal immigrant become diva who admitted her origins even as she masked them in speech and appearance, was to become an emblem of the national soul.

Argentina, a country of immigrants, would have to grapple with the demagoguery of nationalism, on the one hand, and a provincial cosmopolitan opposition, on the other, for years to come as it tried, with variable success, to achieve a certain sense of itself beyond the questionable cachet of being the most European of Latin American countries.

Here's your one-way ticket: The white slave trade

Tango took up decontextualized women as one of its favorite subjects. Its lyrics are fascinated by those who deny their class origins even as they punish luxury and flashiness. Singing about abandonment, the fleeting nature of youth, the vagaries of love, it frequently refers to women who came by boat to Argentina to work as prostitutes. The interest in distance and other customs, the curiosity about the exotic, became focused on the *francesita* or *franchucha:* the petite French woman whose ubiquity in tango lyrics is testimony to the hold that Paris once had on Argentine sensibilities. It was not, then, only the architecture that should have reminded Saint-Exupéry of Paris when he visited Buenos Aires, but a darker, intimate universe as well.

In *Le chemin de Buenos Aires,* published in Paris in 1927, the journalist Albert Londres details his investigation of the booming white slave trade of the 1920s. French pimps, known as *maquereaux,* discovered that it was highly profitable to export young women to Argentina. Poverty and lack of alternatives seem to have been the lot of these young women, who entered the profession with varying degrees of awareness. Typically, a pimp had a woman he called his wife; a prostitute he put in charge of the others, who were his capital. The investment in each woman was a one-way ticket on the boat, plus clothing and food.

At times, things got out of hand: women might become violent, moody, or unwilling to work for a particular pimp. At that point, they were sold or exchanged. Two pimps would get together and arrange a financial deal, normally based on the original investment and expectation of future earnings. The nature of the deal was not always communicated to the women involved. In one case, according to Londres, one pimp encouraged another to seduce his prostitute so that she would think she was the one doing the abandoning.

For the French women coming to Argentina, the process

was not without romantic ups and downs. Their relationship to the pimps involved abnegation, passion, and continuity. Working hard was a proof of love. Tango refers time
and again not only to romantic betrayals, but also to the
peculiar kind of gratitude owed to the prostitute with a
heart of gold.

Because they were picked when very young, the women's
memories of home were of poverty in a place impossibly
far away. Occasionally, a relative in France would get suspicious of money a young woman sent home and decide to
investigate. It would not take long to recognize the business in which she was involved. Londres recounts the case
of one such relative who, after considerable effort and with
Londres's help, succeeded in contacting the young woman
and pleaded with her to return to France, having even
arranged for her repatriation. The woman, however, wanted
to be left alone; she had changed too much and had no
desire to return to her previous way of life.[6]

Foreign women were endowed by Hollywood with
enduring mystery, an exoticism born out of their displacement from their country of origin. In tango, the drama of
suffering and longing is frequently linked to opera and
works of literature. Comparisons are drawn with women of
ill repute, such as the title character of the opera *Manon*, the
heroine of the Dumas play and Greta Garbo film *Margarita
Gautier*, and the *princesa* of the exoticist poem *Sonatina* by
the nineteenth-century Nicaraguan poet Rubén Darío, as
though the departure from home were confirmation of a
previous destiny already inscribed in culture.

Foreign prostitutes—women from Russia, Hungary, and Poland—arrived in Argentina as early as the 1870s, brought by men from their homelands. The port was a major instigator of prostitution, of course, with sailors asking upon arrival to be taken to certain neighborhoods or nearby towns where they would be fairly sure to find *pupilas.*

Policies regarding the practice of prostitution have varied since the early part of the twentieth century. Open brothels and street solicitation gave way to houses with *pupilas.* Cabarets, nightclubs, and theater acts sprang up in the capital and elsewhere in the country. One bizarre event was a tango contest held in the Hospital de Clinicas, a teaching hospital in Buenos Aires, in which medical students danced in the nude with prostitutes and skeletons.

Although prostitutes in Argentina were of many nationalities, when tango names a foreign woman, she tends to be French. The journey from Paris to Buenos Aires is a favorite subject for tango. Several compositions tell of the longing felt by those who are stranded in Paris, unable to return to the homeland (a theme that became popularized from the male exile's point of view by the movies of Carlos Gardel, whose renditions of "Mi Buenos Aires querido" (My beloved Buenos Aires) and "Anclao en París" (Stuck in Paris) continue to define the distance between Montmartre and the Latin Quarter in Paris, and Corrientes Avenue in Buenos Aires.

Enrique Cadícamo, perhaps the most prolific tango poet, portrays the destiny of a character known as Madam Ivonne: "Han pasao diez años que zarpó de Francia /

Mamausel Ivonne es hoy sólo Madam, / la que al ver que todo quedó en la distancia / con ojos muy tristes bebe su champán. / Ya no es la papusa del Barrio Latino, ya no es la mistonga florcita de lis, / Ya nada le queda . . . ni aquel argentino / que entre tango y mate la alzó de París." Ivonne, ten years after having left France, has gone from being called Mademoiselle Ivonne to just Madam; she is depicted sipping champagne and looking sadly into the distance, no longer the pride of the Latin Quarter, with nothing left, not even the Argentine who, between *mates* and tangos, swept her away from Paris. Ivonne, a victim of love, joins the parade of the seduced and abandoned in Buenos Aires, another figure in the gallery of characters that tango offers to define life in the city.

"What does she want? Where is she going?" (*¿Qué pretende? ¿Adónde va?*) asks the male voice in Homero Expósito's *Margo*, about a French woman who returns to Paris, only to realize she no longer can call that city home and so comes back again to Buenos Aires, disillusioned and without hope, of love or anything else: "París / era oscura y cantaba su tango feliz, / sin pensar, ¡pobrecita! . . . que el viejo París / se alimenta con el breve / fin brutal de una magnolia / entre la nieve. / Después, / otra vez Buenos Aires / y Margo otra vez sin amor y sin fe." Margo, like so many women sung by tango, suffers from a wound that cannot be healed. The very trigger of love's entanglements inevitably betrays the one who is entrapped.

Going back is always a mistake, because time is punishing. Tango tells us to examine the faces and the clothes of those we see in the streets of the city, looking for pride and defeat, in order to recognize those who have been or about to leave. Their names do not matter; their stories are woven through and repeated in other faces in those same streets. Although the details may change—the princess in Rubén Darío's poem *Sonatina*, for example, whose mysterious sadness is presented against the backdrop of royalty, has given way by the 1920s and 1930s to the gallery of prostitutes, thieves, and losers of novelist Robert Arlt (and the tangos of Contursi)—the myth of distance exists throughout Buenos Aires neighborhoods.

The repertoire of early female tango singers, notably Rosita Quiroga, contained a number of compositions—of which "Maula" is one of the better known—that disparaged a male lover who did not live up to his obligations. But it is the white slave trade of the first part of the century that gives tango its themes of a woman's lost hope and her ambivalent relationship to the night (the latter a subject of jazz in the United States as well). On the one hand, the night provides an opportunity for celebration and self-invention; on the other, it represents a departure from one's origins and the uncertainties of uncommitted love.

Tango says that the distance between hope and fulfillment is unbridgeable. Stranded in the city, men and women exist neither here nor there, whether they have abandoned their neighborhood, a simpler way of life, or come from far away.

How Foreign Can One Remain?

Immigration anxiety

The Polish writer Witold Gombrowicz traveled to Argentina in 1939 on what he thought was a brief literary visit. As events in Europe unfolded, however, he decided to stay, eventually being forced into a fight for survival in a country where people did not recognize his name and had trouble deciding on its spelling.[1] Gombrowicz undertook the trip, he claimed, out of intellectual interest in the nature of the Argentine national soul, but he soon found himself struggling to establish his reputation in the intellectual life of Buenos Aires. He ended up staying more than two decades.

Buenos Aires at the time had a thriving café-based intellectual culture. Some of the most traditional spots, such as El Molino and the café La Perla, have in the intervening years either disappeared or been transformed, but in the early to mid twentieth century—one of the most exciting periods in Argentine literary history—they were favorite gathering places for such luminaries as the humorist and philosopher Macedonio Fernández, the writers Jorge Luis

Borges and Leopoldo Marechal, Oliverio Girondo, and
the painter Xul Solar. Although some of these cafés still
remain, they are now bright and aggressively modern establishments where the traditional four-hour cup of coffee or
shot of *ginebra* has been replaced by pastries and pizza.

In the heyday of these cafés, Buenos Aires was a cultural
center. Between 1924 and 1927, the avant-garde literary magazine *Martín Fierro* brought together writers and visual artists
in intense collaboration. Its name referred to a nineteenth-
century poem by José Hernández about an Argentine gaucho who wanted to remain free to roam the countryside at a
time when the land was becoming subdivided. The unwav-
ering bent of the group was unmistakable, with their cosmopolitan belief in aestheticism and strong identification
with their European counterparts, as well as their rejection,
through parodies and polemics, of the old-fashioned literary affectations and solemnity of such figures as the poet
Arturo Capdevila, whom they called *Dr.* Arturo Capdevila.

They wanted to be free, like the gaucho in the poem:
fresh, iconoclastic, and new, yet also grounded in tradition.
Those who contributed to this publication were later split
into two groups, Florida and Boedo, defined by their politics: the populist Boedo group was influenced by anarchism
and socialism, while the Florida group was more inclined to
the idea of art for art's sake.[2] In both cases, the protagonists
thought highly of their own role in Argentine national history, their commitment to art and literature, and the impact
of their work. In a country seen as remote by so many, they

considered their opinions and existence to be of paramount importance.

Buenos Aires, at that time and through the 1960s, conceived of itself as a privileged cultural field, and porteños frequently acted with derisive condescension toward outsiders. This trait was famously parodied by the humorist Arturo Cancela in his 1944 novel *Historia funambulesca del profesor Landormy*, a mocking of both Argentine and French culture.[3] The hero, Professor Landormy, is a visiting scholar who gets into hilarious situations stemming from a combination of Argentine snobbishness and his own endless capacity for delivering boring lectures. Witold Gombrowicz, too, frequently scoffed in his diary at the Argentine air of superiority.

Gombrowicz spent a great deal of time in cafés. He became a permanent fixture of some of those establishments—in particular, El Gran Rex and La Fragata—integrating himself into the urban landscape with his battered coat, an idiosyncratic character of aristocratic ambitions but marginal existence. He wanted to be visible and highly regarded while at the same remaining condescendingly detached from conventional recognition. The café culture suited him well in this regard, and was an ideal stage for his dramatic playing out of his foreignness.

His journals bear witness to the feelings of cultural distance experienced by a man whose Spanish remained noticeably awkward throughout his life in Argentina. In 1946, the expatriate Cuban writer Virgilio Piñera met him at El Rex. In his description of their encounter, Piñera relates Gombrowicz's description of his arrival in Buenos Aires, a story that everyone else around the table knew already but that was required listening for anybody wanting his acquaintance.

By then, Gombrowicz attributed his having stayed in Argentina to a study of the South American soul initiated the night before his boat docked in Buenos Aires. The journey itself had been comfortable, with luxurious dinners at the captain's table and all the recognition due to a writer coming on a special visit. By the time Piñera met him, Gombrowicz preferred to be addressed as "Count," even when he was in such monetary need that he had to ask to be invited to dinner by friends he encountered "by chance" in the streets.[4]

When Gombrowicz arrived in Argentina, the most important writers of the moment were being published in the now legendary *Sur*. This journal had been founded in 1931 by Victoria Ocampo, a wealthy woman of letters whose diaries and correspondence remain among the important documents of the era. Victoria was an independent woman who wrote and hosted international literary luminaries in her house and in the pages of the magazine. She also became the lover of a number of her guests, such as the French collaborationist Drieu La Rochelle, whom she befriended despite her own antifascist and anti-Nazi beliefs. Like *Martín Fierro*, *Sur*, in its very title, boasted a local identity while operating within a markedly cosmopolitan frame. Among the results of its cultural self-assurance was the publication of excerpts of Joyce's *Ulysses* before the work came out in book form.

The core group of *Sur* included Victoria Ocampo, her younger sister Silvina Ocampo, and Borges. Silvina Ocampo was married to Adolfo Bioy Casares, Borges's close friend and collaborator. Silvina's detached narratives are among the best of her generation. Dining and partaking of the literary scene in the Ocampo-Bioy Casares homes was a much cherished experience.

It might seem that Gombrowicz, who had the requisite European background, aristocratic pretension, creative originality, and aloofness, fit perfectly in this group's midst. Such, however, was not the case. One afternoon I asked Bioy Casares why they were not closer to Gombrowicz. He told me with an ironic smile that they had little in common. Silvina held a rather amused view of Gombrowicz as a character, and *Sur* was silent about Gombrowicz's most important work, *Ferdydurke* (1937), because they simply did not like it.[5] An attempt to bring him into the fold at a dinner at the Bioys' home that included Borges and other writers yielded no meaningful contact because neither Borges nor Gombrowicz enjoyed conversing in public. (Borges would change in this respect over the years as he became less aware of the number of people in the room due to his blindness.) Silvina's account of Gombrowicz contains an imitation of his diction and faulty grammar as illustration of what she euphemistically called the "differences between their circles."[6]

The most cosmopolitan writers of the country were,

perhaps ironically, also the most profoundly rooted in Argentine customs. They felt that theirs was the best Spanish, which included the right to ridicule others because of their accent; fashion was a target as well, for example the way Gombrowicz wore his shirt unbuttoned, just a bit too low for the Buenos Aires standards of the time. Although Gombrowicz's way of writing may have been too edgy for these classicists, who epitomized Borges's suspicion of innovation and originality, his philosophical bent and theories about the role of writing could have allowed him a place similar to that of Macedonio Fernández, whom Borges touted as his master.

Earlier in the century, Macedonio Fernández engaged in a powerful dismantling of the very idea of a self. In a spirit akin to the philosophical side of Dadaism, he took on the established truths of nineteenth-century literature, attempting through the use of radical humor to convince his readers that their individual identities were mere illusion, born out of a belief in dogmatic forms of realism. Readers, he believed, had been taken in by a literature in which plots based on sex and money diverted them from a metaphysical encounter with eternity. The first step in attaining eternity, in his view, was to overcome the self, which he saw as a superficial notion. If people stopped believing that their identities had any particular weight, they would be able to step out of the constraints of time.

Following up on his teachings, Borges once envisioned a dialogue with Macedonio in which they decided to commit suicide. The dialogue ends with one of the speakers saying that he is not sure whether they in fact managed to take their lives. Whereas the road taken by Macedonio involved puns, neologisms, and manifesto-like pronouncements, the one chosen by Borges gave us parallel worlds, a skepticism about individual identity, and the erasure of difference over time. From a current perspective, Gombrowicz's work should be part of that conversation.

According to these intellectuals, however, Gombrowicz was not in the same league as other Europeans, and so did not belong in their circle. Writers such as Roger Caillois and Drieu La Rochelle, for example, despite their political differences regarding Nazism, enjoyed prestige because they were French, France being a cultural touchstone for Argentines. *Sur* was not about to confuse Gombrowicz with aristocratic expatriates and admired guests. In spite of Gombrowicz's self-aggrandizing view of his landing in Argentina, he apparently remained in their eyes a questionable uprooted intruder.

Gombrowicz may not have been accepted into *Sur,* but he was held in admiration by younger writers, some of whom revered him to the point of proselytism; their hope was that his 1937 novel *Ferdydurke* would be widely known and regarded not as a mere work of fiction, but as a way of looking at the world. *Ferdydurke,* a thoroughly nonpsychological, humorous narrative that favored discontinuity and blurred differences between poetry and prose, satisfied a hunger for a productive antirealism.

The translation of the novel was itself a testimony to the veneration he inspired. A group of writers, presided over by

Virgilio Piñera, worked as a committee in a café to render the novel into Spanish. Adolfo de Obieta, son of the legendary Macedonio Fernández and a poet and essayist in his own right, initiated a subscription campaign to see the novel published. That group understood the importance of what Gombrowicz was doing, and rescued him from the isolation that he both cherished and wished to shatter.[7]

There is no doubt that Gombrowicz wanted to be famous. One of his diary entries reflects on how mistaken Argentines were to hold Borges in such high regard, when he himself was better able to represent their true nature: "They do not know that I am somewhat of a specialist in their main problem—immaturity—and that all of my literature is at home in it. It is paradoxical that in South America, Borges, abstract, exotic, not tied to their problems, is a luminary, but I have only a handful of readers. The paradox, which stops being a paradox when one reflects that they can show off Borges in Europe. Not me because I am a Pole. I am not *valor nacional.*"[8]

Gombrowicz tested those around him in ways that gained him a reputation for arrogance. The men with whom he shared many moments of his life, younger writers, felt seared by his intense criticisms and humiliating comments, even as they regarded him as a master and were much influenced by his thought. Although he was far from a Polish nationalist, it was clear that he was not going to bow down as a guest in a country he felt in many ways was beneath him. Rather than thanking Argentina for its hospitality, rehearsing the rituals of settling down, and planning for the future, Gombrowicz conveyed the sense of being in transit throughout his residence there.

He acted as though he wanted to be alone, but he did so in the very public space of the café, wishing to share his aloofness. One is reminded of Jacques Derrida in *La carte postale* (1980), when he insists, in a paradox of privacy, that he writes in full view of everybody so that his wish for concealment might be understood, thereby forging a secret.[9] Gombrowicz did not want the invisibility of a foreigner; he wanted to be known as a writer and followed as a visionary. But at the same time, he needed to establish a link that he would be free to break at will.

In a city and a country in love with the idea of the individual, he was an eccentric who played his role in public. His jobs, which were varied, he obtained through acquaintances he had charmed into believing in his worth. He worked in a bank, with rather bad results, and taught classes to private groups on a number of subjects that seem trivial but that must have impressed on attendees the originality with which Gombrowicz saw the everyday.

While striving to remain set apart, Gombrowicz became naturalized as part of the life of the cafés and *pensiones* (boarding houses) in which he spent his days when he was not working. The tango *Cafetín de Buenos Aires* (Buenos Aires café), by one of the leading informal philosophers of Buenos Aires, the tango poet Enrique Santos Discépolo,[10] describes this milieu well: "En tu mezcla milagrosa de sabihondos y suicidas / yo aprendí filosofía / y la poesía cruel de no creer más en mí" (in your miraculous hodgepodge of know-it-alls and would-be suicides / I learned philosophy and / the cruel poetry of not believing in myself anymore). Gombrowicz became one of those café philosophers, uprooted, unattached, willing to tell the story of his arrival so that all might realize that he belonged, or at least once *had* belonged, elsewhere.

When Virgilio Piñera told how Gombrowicz recounted his arrival in Buenos Aires, saying that it had the feeling of a rite of passage, he was only hinting at the event's importance for Gombrowicz. In 1953, Gombrowicz published a novel, *Trans-Atlantyk,* that more thoroughly explores his contradictory national and cosmopolitan wishes.[11]

The plot of *Trans-Atlantyk* invites the reader to participate in the same rite of passage that Gombrowicz experienced. In Argentina, he decided to write a novel modeled on an archaic Polish form, written in a stilted, recondite style. The tale is precisely that of the arrival by boat of a Polish writer, Gombrowicz, in Argentina. The characters, his efforts at survival, and the comedy of manners that he describes parallel his life without being autobiographical. *Trans-Atlantyk* is reminiscent of marionette theater: its emphasis is not drawn from affect, but from hyperbole; the transitions are not fluid, but abrupt. Its humor is dark and threatening. And yet, unwittingly, Gombrowicz was associating himself with the powerful Spanish tradition of the *esperpento,* the freakish theater of Ramón del Valle Inclán, the repudiation of self of Macedonio Fernández, and the practice of the absurd of Ramón Gómez de la Serna. He wanted to write in a Polish uniquely his own because of its anachronism, yet ended up being accessible to the Spanish-speaking public because of a tradition of which he was not aware. Those around him, inspired by the sheer energy and depth of his vision, retranslated—both literally and figuratively—his work, thus rendering Gombrowicz's true arrival in Argentina as a productive mistake.

Café fellowship and conversation were at the root of this experience. Despite knowing no Polish, a number of writers, as we have seen, undertook in an act of formidable communion to translate *Ferdydurke* into Spanish, with Gombrowicz's full collaboration. One can only imagine the discussions that ended up yielding particular word choices, in the effort to naturalize the novel. This effort marked Gombrowicz's welcome into the country, the assurance that he would not remain invisible. The friends and associates sought by the protagonist of *Trans-Atlantyk* were, in reincarnation, the admirers of *Ferdydurke*. While Gombrowicz did not succeed in being admitted to the tightly knit circle of *Sur,* he did become a star in café life, with its implied transience. Not a house or apartment for him, but *pensiones;* not the dining table and the literary chat of an established group, but the more occasional and shifting attention of marginal characters coming and going from the establishments he favored. As an exile, Gombrowicz was the male intellectual version of Jean Rhys's aimless female characters. Together, they offer two versions of a newcomer's life in a foreign urban space.

In a recent conversation, Carlos Bruck, an Argentine writer and psychoanalyst who as an adolescent felt the impact of *Ferdydurke*'s vision, told me of a trip he made to Tandil when Gombrowicz was living there, to film the man he considered crucial to his own understanding of the world. Bruck's gravitation toward Gombrowicz the man was not isolated; the faithfulness of those in the translating committee was matched by an Argentine readership that, though small, found in *Ferdydurke* a language of their own.

Not only was *Ferdydurke* no longer foreign; it also took on the very texture of life in Buenos Aires and other Argentine cities.[12] Its games of distancing, its remoteness and sarcasm, the deliberate awkwardness of its flow, generated and portrayed a way of being essential to the lives of those who, not satisfied with the idea of *Ferdydurke* as a mere book, took it as a paradoxical program for action—calling to mind, several decades later, *Hopscotch* by Julio Cortázar, one of Gombrowicz's admirers. Meanwhile, Gombrowicz himself was being absorbed by the ethos of the place, in a turn that approximated Cortázar's relationship to Paris. Exile was an organizing principle for both of them, with a *here* and a *there* that conveys a sense of familiarity and kinship.

Argentine popular culture surrounded Gombrowicz in the form of friends and followers who shared a twin fascination with tango and his writing. Mariano Betelú, a graphic artist whose close friendship Gombrowicz notes in his diary, drew portraits of the self-styled Polish aristocrat at the same time that he was developing a lifelong interest in tango lyrics and scenes. Others, such as Ernesto Sábato, author of *Sobre héroes y tumbas,* would go on to write about the origins and stories of tango. Gombrowicz had quickly become one of the characters evoked by tango, living out his life in cafés, and observing him was one way in which Betelú and Sábato marked his inclusion in Buenos Aires culture. Gombrowicz was more than a foreign author; he had become part of an urban tale.

Gombrowicz may not have been aware of the extent to which loss and longing are inscribed in tango, but in living the dual life of a foreign writer cut off from his original language and community, he reproduced them. A café character himself, evoking the cult of chance encounters and a fatalistic sense of human nature, he had become the very thing that others attempted to understand through their art and writing. In the end, Silvina Ocampo failed to capture Gombrowicz in her imitation of his accent because the most telling aspect of his foreignness was not the awkwardness of his speech, but the perfect fit it represented in Argentina.

Far from the homeland

For Gombrowicz, exile was an encounter with a persona he would not have known had he remained in Poland. By traveling to Argentina, he became an apprentice. One of his diary entries describes how being cut off from his language and community affected him:

> Today I awakened in the delight of not knowing what a literary award is, that I do not know official honors, the caress of the public or critics, that I am not one of "ours," that I

entered literature by force—arrogant and sneering. I am the
self-made man of literature! Many moan and groan that they
had difficult beginnings. But I made my debut three times
(once before the war, in Poland; once in Argentina; and once
in Polish in emigration) and none of these debuts spared me
one ounce of humiliation.

I thank Almighty God he got me out of Poland when
my literary situation began to improve and cast me onto
American soil, into a foreign tongue, into isolation, into the
freshness of anonymity, into a country richer in cows than
in art. The ice of indifference conserves pride quite well.[13]

Gombrowicz felt he deserved more public recognition
than the free-floating café life of Tandil and Buenos Aires
afforded. Although he often noted the blinding effect that
official honors might have had on him, he remained acutely
interested in the critical reception of his writing. By thinking of Argentina as a backwater, and Poland as a land
inhabited by deluded nationalists, he was able to invent
for himself the persona of the lonely aristocratic writer.
Misunderstood, unknown, and disregarded, he achieved
a measure of independence that he portrayed in a self-
deprecatory manner: "In Tandil I am the most illustrious
of men! No one equals me here! There are seventy thousand
of them—seventy thousand inferiors. I carry my head like
a torch."[14]

Provocation is at the root of Gombrowicz's writing;
his thoughts on being an expatriate are in a continuum.
Between 1939 and 1963, Gombrowicz was a thinker of exile.
Arrogance and mistrust of national awards for art and tal-

ent sustained him, even as they cut him off philosophically from any particular land. Yet, in the end, Gombrowicz, who wanted nothing more than to speak to universal concerns, found his voice in an almost constant interplay with specific national geographical spaces.

Poland and Argentina are his reference points for understanding his own condition. Recognition—that is, the knowledge that writer and readers speak the same language, either literally or in the broader sense of sharing and understanding one's thoughts frequently expressed in the form of admiration and awards—was for him both a proof of parochialism and a condition to be coveted. Although he wrote for an émigré journal in Paris and attempted to meet writers in Argentina, he considered himself a swaggering loner whose proof of excellence was to be found in the difference between the stature he merited and his relative anonymity.

Gombrowicz's literature has a staged feeling; his characters seem to strut on the page. His diary has a similar effect. When he says that he carries his head "like a torch," he means that he wants others to look at him in a certain way. His invisibility is a source of pride, even as it creates the possibility of spectacle. *Trans-Atlantyk* opens with a theatrical tone typical of his writing:

I feel a need to relate here for Family, kin and friends of mine the beginning of these my adventures, now ten years old, in the Argentinean capital.

Not that I ask anyone to have these old Noodles of mine, this Turnip (haply even raw), for in the Pewter bowl Thin, Wretched they are and, what is more, like wise Shaming, in

the oil of my Sins, my Shames, these Groats of mine—oh,
better not to heave it to the Mouth save for eternal Curse,
for my Humiliation, on the perennial track of my Life and
up that hard, wearisome Mountain of mine.[15]

He does not seek intimacy. Gombrowicz eschewed the
idea that art and literature existed for communication.
This novel, loosely connected to his biography, recounts his
arrival in Argentina as a parody in which poverty, hunger,
unemployment, the glitter of the diplomatic world, and
the lives of the wealthy appear as a laughable parade. As
for himself: "I Walk, Walk, and he likewise there Walks,
is Walking and the Devil, the Devil!"[16] Indeed, he walks,
carrying his head like a torch, telling what he sees not as
a participant but as a voyeur. The act of walking, whether
it is used to reveal that the experience being described is
already passing away, to describe pursuit of anonymous
contact, or simply to witness without attempting to understand, is ubiquitous in both *Trans-Atlantyk* and his diaries.
Walking establishes the narrator's superiority. He is there at
the moment, but he can always walk away. This is part of a
fleeting reality, we are told; let's move on to something else.
I shall walk and so will the reader.

The lightness of the experience of national borders, created by the very possibility that one can at any instant take
off on a voyage, is part of the Gombrowicz sense of "walking." If it is possible to leave one's country never to return,
everything else becomes a stop in an open itinerary. At
times, this lightness gives way to the manic pace of a Lewis
Carroll celebration:

In a flock they came and in a flock they Dance, hoopla,
hoopla, fiddle dee dee, heels they spark, the whole house
Fill so that into the Park it bursts. Chirp, chirp, with his
children in a chimney Mazur-cricket sits! And in the lake
all the fishes are a-sleeping. Kuling now, Kulig!

> Caught Pann Zenon Panna Ludka, Whirled:
> *Beyond the wood, beyond the glen,*
> *Danced Gosia with the mountain men!*

Here servants rush about with food, with bottles, tables
lay, there Gonzalo gives commands, and coachmen, footmen
peer through windows, and now the whole house Booms so
that into Meadows, into Fields is booming out! Let's drink!
Let's revel, have a drink, why do you not? And another!
Hoopla, hoopla, heigh, heigh, heigh![17]

But this is not Alice's dream; it is Gombrowicz's rendi-
tion of a trip in which something irreversible has occurred.
The voice that creates the dance of the Polish revelers in
Argentina communicates itself as artifice. From the outset,
Trans-Atlantyk lets us know that the arrival in Argentina is
a darkly humorous matter; as a result, the extreme vulnerability of the narrator becomes a joke because he declines
to take himself seriously. The characters he encounters
have the consistency of playing-card figures. We sense that
a game is unfolding here; the conviction that what we are
reading is couched in make-believe does not allow us to
return to the comforts of intimacy.

The Polish characters are Polish in an anachronistically
formal way, while the Argentines, presented in snatches,
show up in the streets of Buenos Aires as though they were

stepping in and out of a cartoon. Banned from dialogue and everyday talk because of the farcical nature of their voices, they join the narrator in announcing that what they say is not for ordinary communication. Instead, they create the peculiar isolation of the absurd.

A voluntary expatriate, Gombrowicz regularly chose to avoid the comforts of common sense that allow for the smooth, mindless flow of situations regarded as cordial. His prose reveals instead a preference for awkwardness, such as characterized his own interactions with people. His diary and the testimonies of friends and acquaintances tell of the many times when he would press embarrassing personal encounters to the limit, such as when a woman, introducing him as a foreign, very well known writer, mispronounced his name and he proceeded to quiz her on its exact spelling and on which of his books she had actually read. The contempt with which he portrayed Poles in *Trans-Atlantyk* was matched in his diary by disparagement of Argentines, particularly in their collective acts of self-congratulation. A banquet for the Argentine painter Raquel Forner—whose work he did not like—and her husband on the occasion of their departure to receive an award in the United States caused him to reflect on the meaning of success within that community:

> I saw them, painters, an entire body of them, talking, lashing each other with discourse, having a holiday. I observed them from the sidelines, from another table in the same restaurant. "One can only wonder," as people say. It is indeed strange to see how a mechanism of degradation becomes one

of elevation in such circumstances. Each of these painters
secretly scorned his colleagues because, well, an Argentinean
brush is nothing compared with a Parisian brush—yet
there, at the banquet, all together, affirming mutual honors,
they became quite like a lion, altogether in one heap they
became a paean to their own honor; and their table rang
with praise, their table seemed momentous, even appealing,
because of the number of persons participating in the act of
self-elevation.[18]

Not *we*, not *our*, but *I* is his choice. He has nothing but
scorn for the Argentine love of Paris and the need to have
talent recognized there first in order to see it among their
own. Tango's fortune was that it had been successful in
Paris; its prominence in Argentinean life testified to the ser-
vile kinship that Argentines felt for Paris. No matter that
the stories of tango were about failed love and betrayal—
their very existence validated the Argentine link to Europe.

Gombrowicz, fascinated by the cult of the national as
foreign, was also repelled by it. He would have liked to see,
in both Poland and Argentina, a self-reliance that rejected
group identity in favor of individualism. For him, the banquet for Raquel Forner exposed ease of celebration as a
symptom of group identity. Better the stridency of the lone
aristocrat, the man without a country, than the hypocrisy
of the heap.

From time to time, Gombrowicz met with Polish intellectuals who were visiting Argentina. His account of one
encounter with an unnamed Polish journalist after the war
reveals his mixed feelings. They met in Buenos Aires, in a

café on Avenida de Mayo, and from the outset Gombrowicz did not like him. The reason? It was five o'clock and Gombrowicz, thoroughly acclimated to Buenos Aires habits, ordered coffee while the journalist asked for vodka. But it was later, when they started to talk, that he realized what was wrong. It was what he termed the journalist's lack of freedom—not because he lived in a police state, but because he would change personas as though he could be different people:

> Where, then, did I find that lack of freedom? In something subtle: in every instance this man felt like a character. For example, while talking about Argentina, he says:
> —Here you've got a dictatorship, right? Not surprising in South America!
> Here he has forgotten his Polish identity, he who knows nothing but dictatorship. He expresses himself as a European, and a proud one at that, since he has arrived all the way here via Paris and London.
> Then, in a confidential tone:
> —Now, look at this! The stores! The superb leather goods! And their jewelry!
> There he goes back to being the poor and humble Pole who—just like all his compatriots upon disembarking in Buenos Aires—open their eyes wide at the shop windows. I ask him:
> —And the cars, where are you at in Poland?
> Self-congratulatory response:
> —Have they told you of the Warszawa model? Very reasonably priced, and what a body! No need to tell you more! It's a beautiful car.

With a gesture of the hand, I point to Avenida de Mayo, swarming with cars.

—No traffic jams like this in Warsaw?

All of a sudden it is as if he had been stung by a bee.

—What are you thinking? That we don't have cars at home? But my dear sir, you are still living from your memories of before 1939! Many things have changed since. We have cars, almost as many as here!

—What? Are you serious? Do you mean that traffic in Warsaw is as heavy as in Buenos Aires?

—Obviously![19]

For Gombrowicz, the journalist's opinions and changes in tone represent the ridiculous contortions of a compulsive actor who is unable to understand what he might be beyond his pose. The proud Pole, the humble provincial visitor to a glittery city, and the detached European follow each other in rapid succession; like an out-of-tune instrument, he cannot strike the right note, the one that will reveal his own voice. Was Gombrowicz himself innocent of these transgressions? Did he manage a consistency that the journalist lacked? He considers the question of authenticity time and again in his writing while adopting the persona of someone who is out of context in his daily dealings.

While he sought to praise and even exaggerate the wonders of Argentina with the Polish journalist, with others he berated the country and the shallowness of its intellectual milieu. Among Europeans, he was attracted to Argentina, but among Argentines he frequently expressed impatience and annoyance. But unlike the immigrant, who makes changes out of a desire to fit in, Gombrowicz carved for himself a balcony, a position of privileged detachment from which he could weigh judgment.

For him, understanding meant discovering flaws. After having spent many years outside Poland, he was happy to report that he understood it better because of the freedom he had attained by living apart from his fellow Poles. While his absence from Poland was a source of pride and lucidity, he still had strong opinions about his homeland. Not being part of that society for decades, he felt, gave him an analytical advantage. He could now judge Poland as he did Argentina. For him, uncovering the truth about a place or a people meant finding the rough edges, the things that didn't work, the lying and posturing.

Gombrowicz was needy when in Argentina; he had very little money and was eager for job recommendations, dinner and housing invitations. He managed to get by while perfecting the position of the nonparticipant. Nothing about him suggested that he was planning to stay for good, settle into a permanent social network, become an integral part of Argentine society. He tried not to belong anywhere, but still he wanted to be recognized as a genius. He was convinced of the importance of his thoughts, though they could never garner the respect he felt he deserved.

The mystique of writers as eccentric, antisocial, and condescending helped carve Gombrowicz's public persona at a time when writing was still one of the roads to stardom. Gombrowicz, unenthused by national pride, remained focused on teasing out various national characteristics from his travels, as though he needed confirmation of himself as somebody who existed beyond geographical limitations. Nonetheless, he remained caught up in the everyday realities of social recognition, in spite of his awareness of the ridiculous, humbling texture of literary and artistic groups.

When he left Argentina for Paris, Gombrowicz realized for the first time—or so it seemed to him—how important Argentina had been. Struck by the full weight of the years he had spent there, he allowed himself to recollect and experience a sense of loss in his departure. Although he was returning to Europe as a much better recognized writer, and he was leaving what he considered the hinterlands, his relationship to Paris was not one of admiration. Entries in his diary show how ugly he considered the French, and how much he resented their orchestrated opinions about art and literature.

Intoxicated by the same feeling expressed by Gardel, Gombrowicz now voiced his disdain for the French and suggested a growing nostalgia for Argentina. Though uncomfortable with the idea of literary groups, Gombrowicz would have liked, nevertheless, to have been at the center of one. His corrosive attitude toward the place he lived until 1963 seems to have changed as soon as he left.

It is not hard to imagine that by the time he died in Europe, in 1969, he had become a full-fledged, ill-at-ease, reluctant Argentine-in-exile, the very type exalted by tango for his foreignness.

The Self and Its Impossible Landscapes

Alejandra Pizarnik

Enigmatic, frequently somber, Alejandra Pizarnik features radical representations of exile as a state of mind. She at once mocks and mourns her own identity, frequently proposing either death or relentless punning as a response to the puzzlement of life.

She was born in 1936 in Buenos Aires to Jewish parents who had immigrated from Eastern Europe. Drawn to the humanities and the arts, she entered the University of Buenos Aires in 1954, where she first majored in philosophy; she then switched to literature but did not complete her degree, choosing instead to study painting with the Surrealist artist Juan Batlle Planas. In the lively and artistic Buenos Aires of the time, the different directions in which she channeled her talents were entirely consistent. Batlle Planas himself had deep links to literature, and connections among the visual arts and written language were frequently stressed in exhibitions, lectures, and readings.

In 1960, Alejandra Pizarnik went to Paris, where she

lived and worked for four years in what turned out to be a crucial period in her development. An avid reader of French literature, she translated works by Antonin Artaud, Aimé Cesaire, Henri Michaux, and Yves Bonnefoy into Spanish and became close friends with Italo Calvino and Julio Cortázar. Though shy, she was nevertheless able to become closely associated with what remained of the Surrealist movement in Paris.[1] Both in that city and back in Argentina, she was an active contributor to several literary and scholarly journals from Europe and Latin America, among them *Les Lettres Nouvelles, La Nouvelle Revue Française, Sur, Zona Franca, Mundo Nuevo,* and *Papeles de Son Armadans,* and she published well-received books of poetry and poetic prose.[2] Octavio Paz, the Mexican poet and Nobel laureate, wrote the preface to her 1962 collection *Árbol de Diana,* hailing her as an original and strong talent. In 1969 she was awarded a Guggenheim fellowship. At a time when poetry was already becoming a marginal genre, Alejandra Pizarnik managed to be recognized as an important writer while also continuing her activity in drawing and painting. Her romantic life, mostly lesbian, is made explicit in some of her poems. In 1972, she took her own life.

Despite the success she attained and the name she secured for herself, Alejandra Pizarnik felt like an outsider, and her writing consistently turned inward to question her own rootedness. She invented a persona dwelling in a space of memory completely cut off from any factual origins. Through her work, the artistic and literary tradition of the avant-garde comes alive as testimony to a radical form of exile. There is no community, friendship, or true love. The intense loneliness of her writing, the way in which her language echoes itself and appears to deny the outside world , is a protracted effort to leave it for good: hers is a poetry of the one-way ticket.

Where is the self?

Who was this woman? How did she view herself? Alejandra Pizarnik was aware of the Macedonio-Borges register and articulated her vision in an idiom that questions from the outset the weight of the visible. Her language prods the palpable and obvious, inviting access to another realm. In her book *Árbol de Diana* (Diana's tree), we read the following lines:

> she undresses in the paradise
> of her memory
> she ignores the cruel destiny
> of her visions
> she is afraid of not knowing how to name
> what doesn't exist (p. 32)[3]

Memory may be a paradise of reassurance, but oblivion and the threat of not making sense are everywhere in her writing. The visions she invokes in her poetry are casualties of the contradictory tensions between the recovery of the past and its erasure by time. Fear closes this section of *Diana's Tree*; here, she speaks about silence and the difficulty of capturing with words an elusive territory of visions that stem from memory. Undressed in that paradise, the *she* is about to become a victim of her own willingness to name that which doesn't exist; a terrible destiny awaits her recollections. Perceiving memory as paradise is, thus, a mistake. Vulnerable, naked, she is suspended between the past, experienced—mistakenly—as paradise, and the future, which will correct any initial optimism with disappointment.

Being a young girl is more than a memory for Pizarnik. The girl is evoked throughout her poetry as a presence, with a materiality that underscores the uncanniness of time. Hers is a longing for a moment in which the self remains unquestioned.

> now
> in this innocent hour
> I and the girl I was sit down
> on the threshold of my gaze (36)

Beyond the poet's control, the girl takes on different existences.

Pizarnik's language is indebted to another avant-garde writer, Vicente Huidobro, who founded a school he named *creacionismo,* in open revolt against literary realism. Very much like Macedonio Fernández, Vicente Huidobro resisted mimetic art. *Altazor,* a long poem that asserts his *creacionista* stands, contains some lines in which he addresses poetry as *señora arpa* (madam harpist) and asks her to stop producing a series of images that he feels compelled to banal inventory. Pizarnik echoes Huidobro's resistance to the commonplaces of poetry in *Diana's Tree* when she writes, "no more sweet metamorphoses of the silken girl / now a sleepwalker in the cornice of fog" (37). The reference is to something almost unimaginable beyond the written page, releasing the energy of language rather than insisting on its capacity to represent the world like a camera. The silken girl sleepwalking in the cornice of fog embodies the elusive nature of writing.

Creacionista image, then, daughter of the avant-garde, this girl is also a memory of somebody who, by her very nature, has no existence in the history of the self as autobiography. Rather, she locates the poet's self in art and literature, granting her an existence in which the familiar in the narrow sense has been displaced by a wider realm of shared words and visions. Pizarnik's poetry finds its definition in uncertainties, elicited by a seesawing between dream and waking life. In a manner not unlike the one found in Borges's ongoing play against univocal identity, as in "Borges and I," *Diana's Tree* suggests a doubling of the individual poetic persona. But unlike in Borges, the doubleness here is seen as a parasitic rivalry:

> Fear of being two
> on the way to the mirror:
> someone asleep inside me
> is eating and drinking me up (47)

Despite the fear of partition, an interiority is affirmed "inside me . . . eating and drinking me up." The cannibalistic other thus acquires names and faces in Pizarnik's poetry. They are the girl *(la niña)*, Madame Lamort, *muerte* (death), *sombra* (shadow), and *la reina muerta* (the dead queen). This conception of the self is determined through a process of estrangement from its own hypothetical origin. The voice retelling the poem is presented as having been abducted:

"to explain with words of this world / that a boat departed from me carrying me away" (37).

Where did that boat go? What are the terms in which it is represented? Visually, the text inspires Surrealist images in the tradition of Pizarnik's painting teacher, Batlle Planas, as well as the Pre-Raphaelite taste for portraying other-worldly young women.

The effort to create a self separate from the autobio-graphical is expressed frequently in Pizarnik's poetry in terms of despair, solitude, orphanhood, and nostalgia for a girl *(la niña)*, but in another, more powerful layer of her writing she poses insistently the challenge as a triumph in battle:

> Strange to wean myself
> from the hour of my birth
> you have built your house
> you have feathered your birds
> you have knocked at the wind
> with your own bones
> you have finished by yourself
> what no one began (37)

In Pizarnik's land, the one to which she gains access by departing from "the hour of her birth," words and images take on the insistence of an obsession (*una idea fija*, as she says in one poem), gaining transcendence over mere philo-sophical inquiry. Unlike other poets of the *idea fija*, with their tendency to bring together philosophy and poetry, Pizarnik offers us a peculiarly tangible representation of the new space:

> Days in which a distant word takes me over. I
> go through those days somnambulant and
> transparent. The beautiful automaton sings to
> herself, charms herself, tells herself cases and
> causes: nest of taut threads where I dance
> myself and cry for myself in my numerous
> funerals. (She is her mirror set on fire, her wait
> in cold blazes, her mystical element, her fornication
> with names growing by themselves in
> the pale night.) (37–38)

Almodóvar, in his film *Háblale a ella* (Talk to Her), portrays sleepwalking and comatose women, caught between living, dreaming, and nonexistence. Pizarnik, much earlier, puts her self in question as though she were writing from within the cloud to which the main character of Almodóvar's film is consigned. Her very identity will become a pawn: "This repentant song, guard behind my poems: / this song contradicts and gags me" (41).

How are we to read if the writer has been gagged? How to hear the music? In spite of her persistent statements about the unreliability of the writing self, Pizarnik produces a remarkably coherent register for her poetry. The adventures of the self in fragmentation are articulated in the idiom of the visual and poetic avant-garde. Perhaps even more intriguingly, her poetry frequently states its relationship to the turn-of-the-century Latin American poetic movement *modernismo*, initiated by Rubén Darío. Darío incorporated an international and frequently exotic set of objects and images into his poetry. Oriental vases, doll-like women, gardens rather than the jungle populate his verses, spun into musical meters that he and his movement introduced into Spanish for the first time. Invoking the *modernista* impulse, Pizarnik locates poetry—*mi canto* (my song)—in a garden *(el jardín)*, while populating her pieces with swans, princesses, and queens, imagery inseparable from the *modernista* poetics, though here conveying a different tone.

Rubén Darío believed that poetry was a medium for the presentation of a reality separate from daily strife. His exotic birds, plants, art objects, and gardens are cast in poems sure of their capacity to create music that entices and seduces readers. Beauty and the music of poetry are united in celebration. In a poem entitled *On a Poem by Rubén Darío,* Pizarnik says:

> Seated at the bottom of a lake.
> She has lost her shadow,
> not the desire to live, to lose
> She is alone with her images.
> Dressed in red, she doesn't look
> Who has arrived to this place
> where no one ever arrives?
> The lord of deaths in red.
> The man masked by his expressionless face.
> the one who arrived to find her
> takes her away without himself.
> Dressed in black, she looks
> She who never knew to die for love and because of that
> learned nothing
> She is sad because she is not there. (90)

The landscape is Darío's own. The princess of his well-known *Sonatina* is now at the bottom of a lake (lakes being ubiquitous in Darío's poetry) and the otherwise uncertain cause of her sadness is addressed: she is alone with her images. In this way, the princess of *Sonatina* has gone from being the object observed and poetically described—as in Darío's treatment—to the subject who stores images within herself; and the man who has arrived, ostensibly the poet, is not her savior, as *Sonatina* paternalistically implies, but death itself. Fond of color, like the *modernistas*, Pizarnik invents a death by color: red death. In *Sonatina*, the one dressed in red is a buffoon who performs pirouettes. Pizarnik sweeps the red away from its ornamental function and makes it literally cover the poem with the intimation of a death that engulfs both princess and savior.

Does Pizarnik rewrite Darío in order to borrow his imagery and so cast him in a new light? Is the ultimate role of the writing self in this kind of poetry one of criticism and dark parody? Such are the avenues she opens up for interpretation.

But there is more. Pizarnik's poem is dedicated to the French writer Marguerite Duras, whose visions frequently approximate those of Pizarnik herself. The exploration of the female gaze and the eloquence of inaction are not only a tribute to Duras but also a correction of Darío's poem. Through Duras, Pizarnik responds to Darío's question in *Sonatina*, "The princess is sad? What is it that ails her?" (*"La princesa está triste . . . Qué tendrá la princesa?"*). The rewriting of

Darío is not intended to monumentalize a writing self, but rather to further strip it of authority.

In abandoning her own biography and offering herself as an untrustworthy first person singular, Pizarnik seems to enter an ahistorical, utopian space. But the scattering of tasks performed by the self in fact produces a different genealogy, articulating the terms by which she may be recognized as part of another chain. Rather than starting from zero, she enters a preexistent domain, a tradition. Within that tradition, her writing becomes part of the continuum of the visual imagery of the Pre-Raphaelites and Surrealism as well as a joke on the literary heritage of the Darío school. The ways in which Pizarnik suggests the undoing of her individual voice are thus at odds with her explicit statements. The fantasy of giving birth to herself through the abandonment of the hour of her birth has paradoxically made her part of a family.

Firmly grounded in an alternative genealogy, even her jokes against tradition confirm her credentials and give meaning to her writing. The self that she so wanted to erase in its biographical form ends up inscribed in the larger family of the avant-garde, intensified by the dialogue with contemporaries such as Marguerite Duras.

Of terror, violence, and humor

Pizarnik's friends speak of a woman with a great sense of humor, adept at jokes. There was also a certain childishness about her, an incapacity to deal with the practicalities of life, that invited others to help and, in so doing, become partners in a suspension of the requisites of common sense. While most of her poetry engages a dark, albeit playful, vision of imaginary spaces, her prose has a different voice. Among her most remarkable texts is one concerning the "bloody countess" Erzsébet de Bathory, whose fictionalized biography by Valentine Penrose, a French writer associated with the Surrealists, appeared in France in 1962 under the title *La comtesse sanglante.*

Pizarnik was fascinated by the life of this woman who was said to have murdered more than a hundred young maidens in order to drink their blood. These events of the early seventeenth century moved Valentine Penrose to describe in detail what she saw as the aesthetic dimension of blood and pain. Reminiscent of the transgressive authority of the marquis de Sade and the murderer Gilles de Rais, the deeds of the "Bloody Countess" appear to describe what female desire might entail. Pizarnik wrote about the countess's loneliness after she was walled in as punishment for her crimes. In a closing passage about her life and deeds, Pizarnik reflects on the unspeakable horror of living.

The countess's cruelty and lack of compassion toward her victims, the violation of their bodies, the ultimate objectification implied by murder—all this fascinated Pizarnik. Pain, both felt and inflicted, rather than the generosity of female bonding, is what defines the nightmarish female world evoked by Penrose. Pizarnik, who refused to psychologize femininity, chose to adopt an apathetic amoral gaze in treating the countess. The writer Julio Cortázar, whom

Pizarnik saw often during her stay in Paris, was struck by the case of the countess as well and included her as a recurring character in his 1968 novel *62: A Model Kit*—a continuation of *Hopscotch*, with which Pizarnik was closely associated.

Pizarnik also wrote short prose pieces. In those texts she engages often in punning and other forms of wordplay, including the redefinition of everyday language through the disassembly of commonplaces. A reader used to the complicities of her poetry, the secretive and subtle tone of her lines, cannot but be startled by the obscenities of her prose pieces. Pizarnik's humor is genital, almost puerile. She delights in making words slide into unexpected, graphic allusions to body parts and sexual positions, fluids and orifices. The little girl wandering in an unnamed garden, the abandonment of the self, the games with death, are not to be found here.

Leonor Fini's representations of the female body and Bellmer's broken dolls suggest, in a serious vein, the nature of female desire that Pizarnik jokingly explores in her prose. The success of her poetry has relegated the prose to second place, but her artfulness at producing a baroque festival of heckling sexual humor puts her on a level with the Cuban author Severo Sarduy, who lived in Paris for the better part of his life. An original voice within the living heritage of the avant-garde, Alejandra Pizarnik explored both sides of laughter through her writing, and was lost in its darker alternative when she decided to end her own life.

Most women associated with the Surrealist movement, including Valentine Penrose and Alejandra Pizarnik, as well as the painters Leonora Carrington and Dorotea Tanning, have been rendered exotic rather than exemplary. They stepped aside, looking on from the margin while they worked. They favored crime over abnegation, and an oblique perception of reality over common sense, consolidating perhaps that way their status as outsiders within the avant-garde sensibility of their time. After all, no matter how edgy the views of male Avant Garde artists, these were still, in their eyes, creatures that departed from their own sense of women as victims rather than perpetrators of violence.

Cruelty and madness were privileged by these artists and writers as ways of consolidating a departure from common sense and a trivial pursuit of virtue. Avoidance of roots and community, the avowal of loneliness in a society understood as radically foreign, made them embrace exile as the very definition of their being in the world. Pizarnik, by intertwining her work with these other women's, was able to write herself into a tradition. Her use of humor implies a wisdom attained through the naturalization of the fantastic, the zigzagging between reality and the uncanny as citizenship in a faltering, unreliable homeland.

Pizarnik inscribed herself in a place that defined her but paradoxically told her to leave, and kept her in exile longing for a fullness of experience that had never been within her reach.

Who Will Speak the Truth?

How do you say it in your own language?

I have long been fascinated by "The Captive," a story by the Argentine writer Jorge Luis Borges, about a boy who disappears after an Indian raid, apparently abducted. Many years later a report of a sighting of a man with blue eyes in the wilderness alerts his family, and they go to look for him, but when they find him, he is unable to understand them. Arriving back at their house, he immediately bolts into the kitchen, sticks his hand in the chimney, and pulls out a small knife he had hidden there as a child. The parents weep with joy: it is a scene of recognition, of homecoming. The man's eyes show joy as well, in his case because he recovered the little knife. Ultimately, the man is unable to live within walls and one day he takes off for the wilderness. The story closes by wondering, "I would like to know if the lost son was reborn and died in that moment of rapture, or if he managed to recognize, like an infant or a dog at least, his parents and his home."[1]

What happened in this story? So much that we want

to know is untold. What did the abducted boy experience as he awakened in a different culture? And what does the recovery of the knife mean? We intuit that this is a tragic story for the parents, who lose their son twice, and a much more puzzling one for the son. He has been able to glimpse his childhood, yet he then takes off willingly for the life into which he was so brutally inducted.

Cultural difference is seen here as insurmountable. Either you speak your native language or you leave your house. The little knife embodies the familiar, but it has lost its eloquence; the intimate but intransmissible identity of the son is now cut off from his family and native tongue. The man does not have the luxury of being between two languages, between cultures. His, the story leads us to believe, is a world of stark choices. Though free, he remains a captive because he is unable to remember the words of his childhood.

This is a bleak view indeed of the consequences of total immersion in an alien culture. Borges, the blind polyglot, passionately interested in the intricacies of translation, practitioner of the art of anachronism and ambiguity, has given us in this tale an antimodernist warning: stay close to home lest outsiders come and abduct you. You risk everything if you leave, and should you return, the pain might be unbearable because you will see your own life for what it is: a profound mystery. You won't even be able to express the value of your most secret possession, and that little knife will remain the puzzle that holds you back from fully belonging anywhere.

The Americas abound in stories of people who had to craft their lives within new languages, either willingly or forced by circumstances. Nostalgia; the fear of losing touch with one tradition by becoming assimilated to another; the sheer freedom of reinventing oneself in a new world, with the concomitant anxieties of self-hatred; and the triumphs of individual creativity versus the obligation toward community are recurrent subjects in today's literary and cultural reflection. Those arriving in the United States, Canada, and Latin America from elsewhere, as immigrants, expatriates, refugees, or exiles with languages other than English, raise the question of who is foreign, and answer it in practice by incorporating their languages and customs into a new idea of the national. The shortening of geographical distance by inexpensive, fast travel and the realities of the new marketplace suggest that the comfort and shelter once produced by speaking in only one language is now to be gained by speaking many.

In order to be good neighbors, friends, and associates, we must interact in languages that once seemed exotic, the province only of academic interest. The fear of being different in the Borges story is clear: others will come and abduct you. The reality of foreignness in today's world is that we are all, to some extent, those others. Instead of taking each other captive and enforcing a silent oblivion of the native tongue, we talk intimately and eloquently in many languages. Those objects we cherish because of their deep links to our daily experience come with labels that say Made in China, in Poland, in Mexico, in the U.S.A., by workers whose languages are not necessarily those of the mainstream societies in which they live. We move around or stay put, but the objects that surround us, the people we live with, the materials of our cities, the fruits and vegetables we eat, all tell a story of travel, of people whose differing cultures are inextricably intertwined.

How far away do we stand from the captive in the story? Borges's reflections on posing, talking, and exile reveal his view of the ironic tricks played by history.

On lies, ridicule, and silence

"What kind of man, I ask myself, conceived and executed that funereal farce? A fanatic, a pitiful wretch, a victim of hallucinations, or an impostor and a cynic?" inquires Borges in "The Sham."[2] He is speaking about a man in the Argentine province of El Chaco who travels with a blond doll whom he casts in the role of Evita's corpse while he takes on the role of grieving widower. Poor people come by to give their condolences, addressing him as "mi general," and he, with "his hands crossed over his stomach in the attitude of a pregnant woman," acts every bit the part. A fee is charged; each pays two pesos for the privilege of paying their respects, which they exercise more than once.

The situation evokes another. After her death in 1952, Eva Perón was embalmed by a Spanish physician, Dr. Ara, and exhibited in her former office at the CGT (Confederación General del Trabajo, or National Confederation of Labor). For almost two years, an adoring crowd came to view what could not have been too different from the doll in the Borges text. But in 1955, after Juan Perón was overthrown, Eva's corpse disappeared. Its absence gave rise to numerous theories as to its whereabouts, news of random sightings, speculations about conspiracies, and sporadic enshrinements of locales where she was believed to be hidden. Dr. Ara's book about the embalming became a best seller. Some even suggested that copies of the body had been made to throw off possible abductors.

Dead, Evita became an even more magnetic source of attraction for mythmaking and reverence than she had been in life. Her body was now woven into the very fabric of Argentina. Her death was the occasion for a formidable show, and her disappearance (until the location of her body was revealed and she was brought back to Argentina from Italy sixteen years later) left a void that only enhanced her power in the political culture of the country. Evita alive had refused the formal leadership offered to her by supporters in the form of a candidacy to the vice presidency. She owed everything to General Perón, she protested in her 1952 autobiography, *La razón de mi vida* (The reason for my life); he was her truth. She existed only for him and through him. Thus, her embalmed body proclaimed the loneliness of death, stripped as she was from the side of her husband. Dead, she attained the individual existence she had refused when she was alive.

In the play-acting evoked by Borges, the man who performs the role of the grieving widower is granted an identity by the blond doll. Roles have been reversed. He is the *general* to the extent that she is Eva's body. People pay to see him as their *general* only because he accompanies the doll. The sterile Perón is about to give birth to his own identity as a widower, all power conflicts between the two members of the couple erased by their new configuration as mute doll and uniformed husband.

Borges, a fervent anti-Peronist, was not among those worshipping the corpse of Evita or sharing in the grief of her loss. Yet something in the story he tells points to a consistent motif in his writing. "The mourner was not Perón and the blond doll was not the woman Eva Duarte," he states at the end of the story, "but neither was Perón Perón, nor was Eva Eva. They were, rather, unknown individuals—or anonymous ones whose secret names and true faces we do not know—who acted out, for the credulous love of the lower middle classes, a crass mythology."[3] This ending elevates the performance from mere money-making exploitation to an act involving the very condition of authenticity. The real Eva Duarte and Juan Perón had fabricated themselves as mythic characters; the false widower's self-presentation is thus in a continuum with that of the historical man. Both are actors; both fake being somebody, masking their anonymity. Those who pay for the performance are not being exploited; they are, rather, participating in an exercise that acknowledges the couple's fictionality. As they further the performance by paying, the visitors become a simulacrum of the Argentine people—but with a difference. We suspect that they were among those who came from all over the country to view the actual corpse when it was on exhibit. By repeating the act, they not only reinforce their own role as spectators but also erase the authenticity of the original experience, which, no longer unique, now takes on the repetitive nature of a play. It is as though the death of Evita allowed Borges to recast an experience that he once conceived as evil, as one that has simply generated a story—much like the play-within-a-play in *Hamlet*.

This story, which may seem incredible to some, Borges says, took place not once but many times in different places at different times. In stating that it may seem incredible, although it really happened, he wants to grant credibility to his own voice as a narrator. *They* may be faking, but *his* account is the truthful representation of the posing. Even though the man who acts may think that he is taking the ticket buyers for a ride, he is being faithful to Perón's own identity; Perón himself was a nobody acting like Perón. The cleansing effect of the realization reinscribes Borges's relationship to Peronism and gives us a clue to his take on lying and performance. We are back to the logic of the samovar and self-invention, as though the intricacies of posing in exile had become alive in the reenactment of national history.

A joke has gone around in Buenos Aires for years regarding the extent to which the persona one sees is an act. Perón is asked by journalists: "General, what do you think of Borges's stories?" His answer: *"Perdóneme, los cuentos los hago yo"*—Excuse me, I'm the one who makes up the tales.

Viewing General Perón as performing a role opened up the possibility of a Perón as disconcerting as the one hidden in his imitator. The actor was thus a redeemer of sorts, implying that Perón was not identical to the political character Borges despised. The reserve of objectivity left here to the narrator is considerable, as he puts himself in the role of a dispassionate observer able to portray both public and performer. Nobody is actually being misled, but rather everyone is part of a spectacle in which support for whatever might be understood as "true" sentiment is absent.

Ironically cautious about not overstepping a line of decorum and measure, Borges portrays in a muted tone characters who are themselves hyperbolic: Pierre Menard, a Frenchman who wants to be both himself and Cervantes ("Pierre Menard, Author of the Quixote"); Funes, who remembers everything in such detail that he is unable to abstract and interpret what he sees ("Funes the Memorious"); an infinite book that can take over the life of its readers yet cannot be burned lest so doing destroy the entire universe ("The Book of Sand"). Yet Menard does not realize that the part of *Don Quixote* he succeeds in writing portrays the book as being the product of an author different from Cervantes, Cid Hamete Benengeli. Like the fake Perón, the fake Cervantes is faithful to the unreliability of the original. As for Funes, in his taking in every detail of reality, he dismisses all of it by being unable to forget, which is what makes memory possible. His remembering is thus a mask for a radical disengagement of memory. And the infinite book is a monster that defies reading by playing havoc with its own tame appearance, enticing the reader into a potentially deadly experience.

How can one fall in love if one is caught up in a web of false identities and impossible recollections? What sort of love is to be found in these mirages? If identity and community are always suspect, how is one to find the stability that allows intimate connection with someone else? The beginning of an answer lies in a short story entitled "The Zahir," in which, uncharacteristically, Borges talks about fashion in spite of despising descriptions of appearance, famously mocking Henry James for using an excessive amount of words to convey his characters.

At the start of the story we meet Clementina Villar, who soon dies. We know that she was a socialite, and that her picture frequently featured in society columns helped create the legend of her beauty. She also practiced a perfectionism that Borges compares with religious orthodoxy and that is tied to the high regard she had for fashion.

> Like any Confucian adept or Talmudist, she strove for irreproachable correctness in every action; but her zeal was more admirable and more exigent than theirs because the tenets of her creed were not eternal but submitted to the shifting caprices of Paris or Hollywood. Clementina Villar appeared at the correct places at the correct hour, with the correct appurtenances and the correct boredom, but the boredom, the appurtenances, the hour and the places would almost immediately become passé and would provide Clementina Villar with the material for a definition of cheap taste. She was in search of the Absolute, like Flaubert, only hers was an Absolute of a moment's duration. Her life was exemplary, yet she was ravaged unremittingly by inner despair. She was forever experimenting with new metamorphoses, as though

trying to get away from herself; the color of her hair and the shape of her coiffure were celebratedly unstable. She was always changing her smile, her complexion, the slant of her eyes. After thirty-two she was scrupulously slender. . . . The war gave her much to think about: with Paris occupied by the Germans, how could one follow the fashions? A foreigner whom she had always distrusted presumed so far upon her good faith as to sell her a number of cylindrical hats; a year later it was divulged that those absurd creations *had never been worn in Paris at all!*—consequently they were not hats, but arbitrary, unauthorized eccentricities.[4]

Clementina, who studiously prepares herself as a character and attends social functions as though they were performances, follows a code of behavior so strict that wearing hats wrongly portrayed as fashionable, fills her with horror. Her adherence to the trend of the moment does not admit personal choice because her decisions go beyond whatever makes her look good.

We read that a change in fortune caused her to switch apartments and move to a lesser part of the city. Unable to accept her reduced social status, she dies. The story would be little more than an amusing view of an Argentine socialite dependent on European vogues if the narrator, Borges, did not offer—after the devastating portrait of Clementina and her death—the following: "Shall I confess that I—moved by that most sincere of Argentine passions, snobbery—was enamored of her, and that her death moved me to tears?"[5] This narrator does not take the same position as the one who related the story of the Perón-Eva show. This time he enters the performance himself, taking on the role of someone who is taken in by artifice even as he perceives it for what it is. That snobbery could be the most sincere of passions speaks to a notion of love that includes ridicule. Not unlike the lover in so many tangos who learns the unworthiness of the love object, this man has been taken in by a pose.

Clementina's act, Clementina *as* an act, seduced Borges, and in looking at her face in the casket, he is witness to a transformation: "Clementina Villar was magically what she had been twenty years before: her features recovered that authority which is conferred by pride, by money, by youth, by the awareness of rounding off a hierarchy, by lack of imagination, by limitations, by stolidity"; and yet, he observes, "no version of that face which had disturbed me so will stay in my memory as long as this one."[6] Looking at her, he experiences an encounter with a peculiar kind of authenticity. Like the general, he is at the side of a dead woman; and similarly, like those who paid to see her, he submits to a power that transcends her own limitations. Her face, purified by death, devoid of the artificiality of fashion, reveals another layer, no less limited and lacking in imagination.

But "The Zahir" is not exclusively the story of Clementina. The title alludes to a coin given to the narrator after he leaves the wake, one that evokes various meanings, from Judas's thirty coins to the French louis, whose picture makes Borges think of the fugitive Louis XVI in Varennes. Rather than a piece of money, the coin serves as a receptacle for his obsession, as the last line of the story makes clear: "Perhaps I shall conclude by wearing away the Zahir simply through thinking of it again and again. Perhaps behind the coin I shall find God."[7]

The narrator's love for Clementina Villar does not make him stumble into obsession. Her dedication to fashion, her desire to change personality and looks every time she gets news from Paris, and her vulnerability when she buys the wrong hat from an impostor posing as a fashion maven all reveal the way in which earnest, honest devotion may lead to ridicule. It is not without a sense of unease that we react to the comic aspect of her dying because she cannot stomach living in the wrong neighborhood. After all, her life is framed by another obsession regarded as illustrious, the one about a coin that contains its itineraries, a transhistorical object capable of embodying a terrifying set of associations, an emblem of time and space. She had the right intensity but somehow channeled it into the wrong object.

Borges's lighthearted declaration of love for Clementina seems almost a statement of style. We know that they could not love each other with the same dedication that she devoted to fashion or he to the zahir. Only when he is looking at her face in the casket does she somehow approximate, though in a debased manner, the various meanings—the transformations—of the coin. Clementina was not herself unless she could be constantly redefined by fashion. A martyr to snobbery, her end brings a mild reaction from Borges-turned-narrator, who speaks without self-deprecation of his obsession with a coin that is not one.

Borges, like the general, has access to the mystery of death as he stands watch by a dead woman. The innumerable appearances of Clementina in life are nothing compared to her transformations as a corpse. Like the public who went to see Evita lying in state, Borges uses his experience with Clementina to make an intimate discovery.

Things that can change you in dangerous ways are to be distinguished from those that have a merely cosmetic effect. Fashion is an especially clear culprit of superficial change; that is why Clementina (or Eva) is less in her transformations than is the zahir, a coin. The masks of an object that represents others while hiding behind a modest exterior are for Borges of a different nature from other, debased forms of change. Between lying, posturing, and the aristocracy of the enigmatic lie distances both subtle and elusive.

The most privileged object in Borges's work is the Aleph in the story of the same name. The plot features two men, the first-person narrator, Borges, and a mediocre, award-winning poet, Carlos Argentino Daneri, both of whom are interested in the universal. Daneri writes a poem in which he attempts to summarize the universe, while Borges finds in the cellar of the house in which they meet an object, the Aleph, that contains in it all the universe. Untranslatable, the Aleph—kept secret by Borges from Daneri—fills Borges with awe, in a moment of privileged perception that has all the attributes of a borgesian truth since it cannot be encapsulated by language, only alluded to through the retelling of an experience. Indeed, the experience obsesses Borges for some time, but eventually, becoming convinced that what he found is in fact a false Aleph, he is able to resume his normal life.

Carlos Argentino Daneri and Borges are brought together by the death of a woman they both coveted, Beatriz Viterbo. The faithfulness to her memory is puzzling. Photographs of her offer these unremarkable images: "Beatriz Viterbo wearing a mask, during the carnival of 1921; Beatriz at her First Communion; Beatriz on the day of her wedding to Roberto Alessandri; Beatriz a little while after the divorce, at a dinner in the Club Hípico; Beatriz with Delia Marcos Porcel and Carlos Argentino; Beatriz with the Pekingese which had been a present from Villegas Haedo."[8] Beatriz Viterbo, it seems, is an upper-class Argentine woman whose effect on the two men bespeaks the limitations of the experience of love in daily life. The narrator expresses relief at her death: "Now that she was dead, I could consecrate myself to her memory, without hope but also without humiliation."[9]

In both "The Zahir" and "The Aleph," the women love objects manufacture personas that successfully seduce Borges, but not as much as the zahir or the aleph themselves. While the zahir remains true to its changing nature, the aleph that the narrator finds in the basement is false, he ultimately states with relief. Why the relief? Because otherwise Borges would have been forever caught up in its web.

It is fitting that Clementina Villar and Beatriz Viterbo are both dead and counterfeit in a mundane way. Had they been any more "authentic," love would have been monstrous (that is, all-pervasive, obsessive). Borges's musings on the subject culminate in the story "The Intruder," about two men in the Argentine countryside who, infatuated in the same unworthy woman, almost sacrifice their relationship.

The serenity of a perfect community is destroyed by someone who does not belong: a female intruder. She is an outsider, with damaging influence on an otherwise stable world. Like the women evoked in the tango "Malevaje," the intruder represents a disturbing sexual message, but while the tango uses irony to express discomfort over her sexual appeal, Borges's story takes a different view. Here, male friendship is the ultimate good to strive for; thus, when one of the brothers murders the woman, the reader understands this as a happy ending because it brings peace back into the male world. While "The Aleph" and "The Zahir" propose a quest that is isolated and rife with the mirages of lying and ridicule, "The Intruder" takes the role of the female as trouble a step further, enticing the reader to become an accomplice as resolution is achieved through a brutal murder. Life has been cleansed of a foreign influence. The removal of the intruder both seals the brotherly bond and identifies women as the ultimate outsiders in a male order.

Yet the political scenario explicit in "The Sham" exceeds matters of secondariness, faulty representations, and humor. Instead it questions how deeply committed certain characters are to a given historical and political moment.

Borges, an anti-Nazi , was most interested in a particular historical moment: World War II. During Perón's ascension to power in 1945, Borges supported an unlikely coalition, the Unión Democrática (Democratic Front), which brought together conservatives and Communists to oppose Perón in the name of antifascism. In his writing, Borges engaged the issues of death and victimization in a way that blurs clear-cut political stances. The same can be said regarding his attitude toward Perón, which, though uncompromisingly antagonistic, allowed him to reflect on the nature of individual identity and posing, as can be seen in "The Sham."

Two other stories, "The Secret Miracle" and "Deutsches Requiem," further explore the theme of an individual's capacity to state a truth and act in a limited historical situation. "Deutsches Requiem" relates, in the voice of a character named Otto Dietrich zur Linde, the beliefs of a devoted Nazi on the eve of his execution. Being devoid of guilt, he does not ask for forgiveness. Rather, he enumerates his tastes in a dispassionate tone—Brahms, Schopenhauer, Shakespeare, Nietzsche, Spengler—and notes that he wants all those who admire them to know that he shares in the wonder at their work. This moment insinuates Borges into the story since these are crucial names in his own genealogy as a writer.

A classic, Borges says in *Other Inquisitions*, is a text that keeps recurring in the hopes and discussions of a community. He can imagine, he adds, drawing the same implications and associations from works in languages he does not know, suggesting that foreignness of experience need not impede the power of a text to reflect the human condition. In "Deutsches Requiem," he suggests that the reinterpretation of the shared classics—the canon—involves us inextricably and intimately with the enemy in our midst. In this sense, Otto zur Linde's adherence to the Nazi Party stems not from passionate comradeship, but from true conviction: "I will say little of my years of apprenticeship. They were more difficult for me than for others, since, although I do not lack courage, I am repelled by violence. I understood, however, that we were on the verge of a new era, and that this era, comparable to the initial epochs of Islam and Christianity, demanded a new kind of man. Individually my comrades were disgusting to me; in vain did I try to reason that we had to suppress our individuality for the lofty purpose that brought us together."[10]

Otto zur Linde faces death not as a murderer who justifies his violent instincts and social resentments through ideology, but as a dedicated Nazi whose deep historical conviction is based in the same philosophical sources by which Borges defined himself. He describes his diligence as subdirector of the concentration camp at Tarnowitz, and, while mentioning Whitman and Shakespeare, tells how he drove to suicide a Sephardic Jew named David Jerusalem because that seemed the best way to destroy the compassion he felt for him. A convinced Nietzschean, he expects the advent of the New Man and refuses to see his crimes as self-indulgence; they are, rather, a form of abnegation, of self-immolation: "Many things will have to be destroyed in order to construct the New Order, now we know that Germany also was one of those things. We have given more than our lives, we have sacrificed the destiny of our beloved Fatherland. Let others curse and weep; I rejoice in the fact that our destiny completes its circle and is perfect."[11] He feels that because its enemies have adopted Germany's own methods of violence, Germany has in fact won despite its defeat, though the victors do not know it.

The story leaves no doubt that Otto zur Linde is telling the truth about himself. He has no need for posturing and lying. But is he telling the truth about what made him what he is? Is the party what he says it is? Are those texts that contributed to his most intimate perceptions and thoughts actually saying what he reads in them? From his point of view, the victors are lying when they state their opposition to Nazism; without acknowledging it, they are simply confirming the view of history against which they fought.

Otto zur Linde is voicing a deeply held opinion. No posturing here. But in his authenticity, he may be mistaken about Shakespeare, Schopenhauer, and Nietzsche—the very names with which he has built his identity. Whether right or wrong, his sense of who they were and what they believed has directed him onto a path that others with similar personal investment question. The truth that Otto zur Linde is able to tell about himself does not illuminate anything but his own circumstances, though it is strong enough to justify his destiny and, in his view, give a full account of the course of history.

Another story, "The Secret Miracle," looks at history and personal fate during the same period from a different perspective. This time the main character, Hladik, is awaiting execution on charges of philosemitism. A middle-aged writer and scholar, Hladik has been working on a play, *The Enemies*, but he had been unable to finish it. Distraught by the possibility of dying without completing it, he says to

God, "If in some fashion I exist, I am not one of Your repetitions and mistakes, I exist as the author of *The Enemies*. To finish this drama, which can justify me and justify You, I need another year. Grant me these days. You to whom the centuries and time belong."[12] Although the execution takes place on schedule, Hladik is able to finish his play, for he experiences a plenitude and density of time such as he had never known before.

Hladik's play *The Enemies* is rendered possible by his executioners, his enemies. Like Otto zur Linde, he dies having turned his demise into a triumph. For his executioners, he was merely a victim; yet he was able to realize what he had always wanted. Unlike the other characters we have encountered, these two doomed men lived without any element of posing. Both had a direct, unmediated relationship to their goals. One cannot but think that they were truthful. And yet, being truthful, anchored by a stable identity, is not enough.

The German who believes he has won the war and the philosemite who triumphs even as he is being murdered bear their destinies as secrets. To all eyes, these men have been defeated. Yet what these stories tell us is that we do not know how history is lived and interpreted by those who make it. The opposing groups die or triumph blind to the true nature of the conflict, and no amount of individual authenticity can make up for the radical ignorance of what is at stake.

While those granting meaning to their own individual lives may succeed, the context in which they do so is an illusion born out of their personal interpretation. The others, poseurs such as Clementina, Pierre Menard, and Perón, invent themselves time and again, through fashion or misrepresentation, even in death. Truth, however, does exist somewhere. Not in what participants in an event think or say, but in certain objects.

The aleph embodies the most desirable truth, which may encapsulate time and space, but it is also subject to secondariness, since it may be a fake. The zahir, for its part, is perfect, but as a consequence it is inassimilable, one of those truths in the realm of the unspeakable, like the name of God.

Once one finds the truth, silence is the best route to follow, for language leads only to gossip, misrepresentation, and error. Philosemite, Nazi, and Perón become hollow in the logic that holds them to their role. Borges says somewhere that no character can ever surpass the moral imagination of its author. This may explain why he left his most urgent questions pending, in the form of a hypothesis of silence and the absolute. Nevertheless, it is in Argentina where it all comes to be both entangled and unraveled.

Borges considered common roots to be somewhat banal, making a productive joke of it by simultaneously affirming both his non-Argentine origins and his sense of ownership in the history of the country. In the gallery of exiles, captives, guests, and intruders explored in his work, we discover a place sometimes as local as the street corner where he was born or as universal as the imaginary library in which all the books ever written are housed.

I remember his voice. He had a *porteño* accent, spoke in low tones creating a sense of intimacy, especially when, as the blind frequently do, he would hold your arm to make sure you were there next to him. His message, however, was frequently disquieting. When he talked to you about tango or Macedonio Fernández, mixing such references with Emerson, Carlyle, or Schopenhauer, he was letting you know that what you had thought was near, your patrimony, had to be translated, rephrased, in a context that required a voyage.

In order to understand your home and be part of it, you had to have been elsewhere, just like its inhabitants and all its literature, wherever it originated. As a reader and writer he showed us that home, within grasp and yet unattainable, is both a goal and the remains of an elusive, changeable past.

Instructions for Taking a Leap

In the city and beyond the books

Julio Cortázar left Argentina for Paris in 1951, where during the next decade he became part of a group of writers that included Carlos Fuentes, Gabriel García Márquez, José Donoso, Mario Vargas Llosa, and Guillermo Cabrera Infante, among others, that came to be known as the Latin American Boom. The cultural debate during the late 60s and 70s, inspired by the Cuban Revolution, tended to question authors and artists who lived outside their countries because of their supposed lack of engagement in political activity. Cortázar, however, openly supported leftist political causes in both Europe and Latin America, and he identified his literature with the need to break from the written and delve into lived experience.

It is perhaps because of his discomfort with the finished piece, or even with the idea of literature itself, that he is still so well liked by young readers. In some of his writings he invented a language and an attitude that bracketed common sense. He created imaginary characters, the *cronopios, famas,* and *esperanzas*—immigrants to the world of literature whom he brought in through short fictions and naturalized for a whole generation as representative human types. *Cronopios,* touchingly naive, failed to understand things properly and let themselves be guided by enthusiasm rather than self-interest. *Esperanzas,* who tended to be librarians, were quiet and unassuming. Together they conveyed the idea that comic strips, realistic representations, and humor were inextricably linked and that *cronopios* and *esperanzas* were relegated to a corner of the world, which was ruled by ambitious, business-oriented *famas.*

Cortázar's success bridged the distance between literature and experience, in part by his refusal to stay local in his references. In his work, Paris and Buenos Aires, London and Berlin, mingle to form a free-floating *zona,* an area that reinscribes geography as a dreamlike continuum. This concept was aptly illustrated by Julio Silva, a painter and sculptor who collaborated frequently with Cortázar, in a map he designed for the cover of Cortázar's novel *62: A Model Kit.* In it streets from Berlin, London, Buenos Aires, and Paris weave together as though they are all part of the same territory, allowing far and near to converge in a plane where exiles feel at home beyond national borders.

Speaking in "cortazariano," an idiom full of neologisms, bestows membership in an iconoclastic group. Having attitude, creating and being created by a pose—as Gombrowicz did when he insisted on being addressed as "Count," as Jean Rhys's characters do with their clothing, and Manuel Puig did through the sharing of Hollywood fantasies—allows access to an ever-changing array of identities. Sometimes the self-styling seems liberating; at other times, nostalgia takes over as an original moment of plenitude remains stubbornly beyond recall.

Once criticized in Argentina, Cortázar is now seen as having incorporated a disjointed vision of cultural identity into his writing. For many, he is the antidote to Borges's bookishness; to others of a newer Argentine sensibility, he is Borges's true partner in the pantheon of Argentine letters, one of the nation's best-known exports together with tango and beef.

Where is life?

Cortázar's 1967 novel *Hopscotch* pulsates with images of exile and displacement. It has two different readings: one is linear, while the other asks you to skip from chapter to chapter, as in a game of hopscotch. The book is an invitation to take a risk, and it turns reading into a game that, like being thrown into a foreign city, may prove to be a redefining experience.

In *Hopscotch*, life is always about something else, its energy forever weaker than that which propels it.

> Life as a *commentary* on something else we cannot reach, which is there within reach of the leap we will not take.

> Life is a ballet based upon a historical theme, a story based upon a deed that once had been alive, a deed that had lived based upon a real deed.

> Life, a photograph of the noumenon, a possession in the shadows (woman, monster?), life, pimp of death, splendid deck of cards, ring of forgotten keys that a pair of palsied hands degrade into a sad game of solitaire.[1]

Life is a shrinking back, a race in which we are running against the odds because we will not be able to approach the outer limits of knowledge and pleasure. The lack of speed, of intensity, is seen here as self-imposed, and transgression becomes the mode of being for those whose own existence is defined by a need to deepen an exploration they cannot even name. *Hopscotch* tries to make us aware of the numbing horror of common sense by setting up, without facile optimism, the uncomfortable and guilty condition of exile and marginalization as a way out from the blinding effect of the everyday.

How do we get out of the box? What is there to follow the refusal to engage in the mainstream? *Hopscotch* celebrates physical proximity, caresses, frictions, and heterosexual love-making as privileged entry points for intuiting the boundaries of reality. Love's entanglements and misencounters may conquer the narrowness of individual identity, triggering a new economy of dreams that flow freely from one person to another and overcome the fictions imposed by self-preservation. Echoing the faith placed by the Surrealists on the necessity of arbitrary encounters, the oblique love relationship between Horacio and La Maga in *Hopscotch* points to the links between art and experience.

La Maga, absent-minded, a bad mother, and a lover whose desirability is acknowledged by many of the male characters in *Hopscotch*, circulates in the book with the gifts of intuition and naïveté. Her way of knowing may be glimpsed from her tears when she sees certain paintings and her attachment to naturalistic fiction. La Maga is embarrassed by her tastes, which she views as cultural limitations that separate her from the other characters. Yet it is precisely this quality of seemingly always being elsewhere that makes her fresh and attractive to Horacio and his intellectual friends, who simultaneously long for and reject that which she embodies so unproblematically.

La Maga's world has the seductive capacity of naturalism. The death of her son, Rocamadour, is kept a secret from her by her friends because they have no words to face the event. They remain silently in the room with her, watching her tense expectation. She is the sole owner of her suffering. Her friends do not speak in the language of feelings; they will not say anything that might interfere with her personal understanding of a situation they cannot fully grasp. Before realizing that Rocamadour is dead, La Maga writes him a letter on a mirror fogged up by a pot of simmering borscht. It is unreadable, a letter on water, the most ephemeral kind of writing. Yet even if Rocamadour were alive, he would not have been able to read it because he is a baby.

La Maga has no desire to do anything enduring that would suggest something beyond herself. Such is also her relationship to books and art. She consumes without being consumed and without the urge to produce. She cannot take the leap longed for in the novel because she can only perceive herself being exactly where she is.

La Maga is sought after and desired throughout the novel, commented on by others, discussed, and evaluated. She embodies individual identity as a scandalous secret that keeps her tied to the name she now uses, while the one she received at birth, Lucía, is rendered virtually invisible by the self she has created in Parisian exile. She has, moreover, the kind of anachronistic charm that gives authority to her silence and makes the rest of the characters seem lighter, less substantial in comparison. If we want to deepen our understanding of them, we must seek out the things that they reference—books, photographs, paintings, favorite music. We must *research* them, whereas La Maga creates the illusion that she is a full-fledged presence whether on or off the page.

La Maga succeeds in conjuring the feeling of home wherever she is. Surrounded by exiles and expatriates who have lost their compass, La Maga appears to hold a key to naturalness. Her self-assurance places her here and now, devoid of the artifices triggered by culture and displacement. Far from Uruguay, her own country, she is more thoroughly open to adventure than are her counterparts because she does not perceive herself as unfinished and needing to learn from books.

Throughout *Hopscotch*, a profound disappointment with literature is voiced: "Is that not literature again?"[2] It is as though the book is trying to cancel its own words, whether by giving alternative ways to read them or by evoking the hopscotch metaphor, so as to allow the words to say something different. Indeed, and somewhat paradoxically, the most intellectual characters in the book turn out to be the least prepared for undertaking the challenges it proposes. La Maga infuses interest in reading the novel for plot and is, therefore, granted ready access to a perceived deeper experience. *Hopscotch* denigrates literature as secondary and vicarious even as it looks with antipathy toward the kind of projection into the book that confuses literature with life. The epistemological leap proposed by the theoretician Morelli in chapter 62, to an anti-psychological, anti-mimetic art capable of dismantling illusions about the self, fails because even the most intellectual characters in the novel frequently ask to be read as representing life.

The reader's options, variously inventoried, discarded, or adopted by the book's characters, turn the public into participant and attempt to uncover its face. In this sense, *Hopscotch* teaches, dismantles illusions, and suggests literary interpretation as a closed circle. It is an open novel, it has often been said, perhaps the most radical example of such a genre, but if that be the case, it is also an enigmatically controlled work that attempts to guide interpretation by showing us the rules governing the interplay among its constitutive parts. Through La Maga and Berthe Trepat, a sleazy counterpart to Morelli, we are presented with the *tangible,* the body in proximity to pleasure and degradation. Those readers caught up in their web suffer as the book issues an invitation to others who are unwilling to give themselves up to the feelings elicited by fiction. It is inhabited by overintellectualized characters such as Ossip and Horacio, who induct readers adept at theorizing into their uncomfortable club for the unfulfilled. Not unlike Borges in "The Aleph" enjoying the intricacies of the counterfeit, Ossip and Horacio delight in the obstacles to their search for meaning. Cut off from their countries of birth, they celebrate knowledge as collage and exile as a general condition valid both geographically and psychologically.

As the novel takes us from Paris back to Horacio's native Argentina, Horacio encounters his friend Traveler, and they hold a conversation marked by the humor of César Bruto, whom Horacio quotes: *"Si a París vas en octubre no dejes de ver el Louvre"* (if you want Paris in October to move'er, don't forget to see the Louvre).[3] The conversation is as improbable as the rhyme of words in the different languages. César Bruto's wisdom consisted in forcing jokes through errors of spelling and pronunciation that celebrated ignorance regarding the workings of language. The laughter elicited by his humor is liberating, for it allows illiteracy to creep into reading and save the text from solemnity. Its mechanisms are crucial to the understanding of Cortázar's goals in *Hopscotch*.

César Bruto always tells at least two stories: one is to be read out loud, so that even faulty spelling allows the words to be recognized; another is forged as the language reveals its fluidity and the stubbornness with which it lapses into sound that betrays intended meanings. César Bruto urges us to lighten up by surprising us with the arbitrary nature of words, which in turn mock our attempts at serious discursive reflection. Cortázar admired César Bruto and Macedonio Fernández for their use of the kind of humor that erodes the authority of institutionalized literature.

Hopscotch tries to avoid the pitfalls of solemnity by calling on César Bruto's strategies. Horacio (whose own name starts with *h*) rewrites words with an initial *h*—translated into English as *wh*, which succeeds in conveying the artifi-

ciality of the original Spanish when he wants to reinscribe
his personal situation:

> He had been revolving about the great affair, and the incon-
> venience in which he was living because of La Maga and
> Rocamadour made him analyze with increasing violence the
> intersection where he felt he was stuck. In cases like that
> Oliveira would grab a sheet of paper and write down the
> grand words over which he went slipping along in his rumi-
> nations. He wrote, for example: "The great whaffair," or
> "the whintersection." It was enough to make him laugh and
> feel more up to preparing another *mate*. "Whunity," whrote
> Wholiveira. "The whego and the whother." He used this
> *wh* the way other people used penicillin. Then he would get
> back to the matter slowly and feel better. "The whimportant
> thing is not to become whinflated," Wholiveira would say
> to whimself. After moments like this, he would feel able to
> think without having the words play dirty tricks on him.[4]

What kind of dirty tricks could words *play* on him in
a book that borrows its very title from children's play and
invites readers to join in? And what would be entailed in
winning a battle over language? *Hopscotch* is traversed by the
imminence of a punishing laughter, capable of obliterat-
ing all participants in the situation by denying them the
possibility of being taken seriously, that is, at their word.
Laughter cancels out the transparent capacity of language
and unmasks it, instead, as a style lapsing into ridicule.

The most intense moment of humiliating ridicule in
the novel occurs at the concert by the aging Berthe Trepat.
Horacio stumbles into it by chance, a scenario familiar to

readers of Cortázar's short stories, frequently presenting a turn of events in which a character with a ticket to a certain spectacle is shocked to find himself trapped in an unexpected situation that makes him lose the detachment of the ticket-holder. Trepat is incapable of perceiving herself with the parodical distancing of the *wh*. In spite of the fact that her concert follows the aesthetic prescriptions of Morelli in chapter 62, she is laughable. While Morelli's project is unharmed by its relationship to his physical appearance, Trepat is described in hyperbolically physical terms: she is old, deteriorated, ugly, obscenely seductive. Her tastes and pleasures condemn her; they put her, like a freak, in a window display. So intense is her presence that Horacio suffers her contagion; their encounter, the insistent rain, and the homosexuality of the man with whom she shares her life are seen as telling, sinister elements of Horacio's loneliness in Paris.

Without the generous, celebratory laughter of César Bruto, *Hopscotch* uses disgust as a distancing strategy and invites readers to join in the condemnation and punishment of Berthe Trepat. Initially, Trepat might be understood as a trivially grotesque image, and the vertiginous black hole opened up by the revulsion she triggers might appear as a mere naturalistic ornament. But it is not so: Trepat, La Maga, and Morelli stand firm, each defending the uneasy equilibrium of the narrative stratum they represent. Of the two readings suggested by the novel, one linear and suggestive of a plot in which Horacio and La Maga are romantically intertwined, and the other avoiding linearity by giving us numbers to follow, thus preventing us from feeling we have gone from A to Z, we end up wishing to stay longer in each. It is as though each time we get attached to one level of the novel, we have to abandon it, packing our bags and taking off for another one. Just as we have become used to the language of ordinary life in which La Maga resides, we are taken to the theoretical preoccupations of Morelli, who writes in a different register. In this way, the novel suggests an exilic perspective as it elicits various effects of nostalgia, of being lost and trying to get back to a place we think we understand more fully.

Skipping and zigzagging, *Hopscotch* tries to direct readers in the placement of its *wh* by signaling moments in which seriousness and the illusion that language is natural should be avoided. We know, though, that this is not the way in which truly risky games are played. *Hopscotch* does not succeed in avoiding the gnawing humor that it proposes. Thus, some of the literary and artistic theories it posits with complete seriousness are swept away by parodical energy.

The initial celebration of *Hopscotch* was a response to its shuffling of diverse levels of discourse as it favored unions of dissimilar elements in kaleidoscopic dialogical combinations. Morelli's third eye, offered as the alternative to conventional psychology, favored the idea that *Hopscotch* was not merely a novel but also an antinovel, a book to be disassembled so that it might better point toward its own principles of articulation, even as it illuminated how all other novels were made. It came with its own explicit theory, in which each of the fictional levels is bent on referring to another—

an execution, perhaps, of the fiction in metaphoric chains intuited by Macedonio Fernández.

César Bruto's dismantling energy is not as easily contained. Once unveiled, its movement still prevents the reader from winning in the game it generates. *Hopscotch*, a novel with so much chatter, so sympathetic to distraction that the chosen place of reading is undoubtedly a busy café, is imbued with a humor capable of obscuring and reinscribing the greater part of its contents. Through César Bruto we may see theory as a joke; our laughter is a celebration of a theoretical framework always in flight from itself. In rereading César Bruto today, it is evident that he left an important mark on Argentine culture: he signaled the problems that come from monumentalizing "good" language and set about erasing the distinctions between high and low, thus preparing us to understand Cortázar, Puig, and some of the authors that followed. César Bruto made us aware that translating one level of culture into the language of another by practicing the faulty spelling and word articulation, is liberating.

From such a perspective we can denaturalize rules and fight authority. César Bruto's energy is not so different from La Maga's, for both suggest that we need to be outsiders in order to better understand where and who we are.

What is today most readable in *Hopscotch?* Which representation, among the multiple versions it suggests, is most akin to our sense of exile? Once the reader has been saved from naturalistic and realistic somnolence, has uncovered the pretense of academic claims and is ready to take a leap into freedom, the book acquires an unintended meaning. Morelli's deliberately abstract projects, the conversations among Horacio and his friends, the ever-parenthetical relationship between thought and action, now inhabit the growing museum of avant-garde artifacts—a recognizable stock that has lost part of its capacity to startle because of its proliferation in other media and works.

But another vast area of the novel insists on being read. It gives us Horacio's walks in the city, descriptions of streets, the sound and color of words used in conversation. The intense physiology of thought is understood as something alive, embodied in cafés, in the touch and the frictions of lovemaking, in the shapes of beds and the music exchanged. Such are the lives of the exiled characters in a cosmopolitan and difficult city, with their mixed accents, caricatures, Trepat's bad breath, the bottles glimpsed in Horacio's neighbor's room, all of which are part of their relative failures. The fear of unfamiliar cold, the persistent humidity of the *métro* in winter, the evocations of distance, the *here* and *there* created by words, are a key to the emergence of these itinerant characters as uncomfortable but willing city fixtures. The enduring presence of the avant-garde consists in this uncanniness at the very heart of experience and in the paradoxical sense of disengagement that it has incorporated into our gaze. By carving out a place that is forever on the margins, just as it refused and unmasked the illusions of the mainstream, the avant-garde gave citizenship to the experience of exile.

The awareness of this reading invites us to play *Hopscotch* again by entering a rule that appeared to be excluded: put on the *wh* in Morelli's interventions and reject his projects so that we may restore energy to the layer of the novel he wanted to overcome. Is this not a betrayal of the program that *Hopscotch* set out for itself? Are we not playing dirty in suggesting that nostalgia may sum up the quality of rereading as recognition?

The porous nature of *Hopscotch* allows us to slip into its *before* as an *after.* Hospitable, but also obscure and vertiginous, the book keeps on fighting complacency. The echoes of the characters, their voices assimilated as enigmatically present, wink at us as they erase Morelli from the interpretive landscape. The leap that we will not take, that call to a life with a sure, unproblematic depth, may have had as a destination something that was not to be found either in books or in exile. *Hopscotch* prepares us, trains us, and urges us to figure out how to get into the city, beyond the books, while it lets us know that we will have to rehearse the road time and again, as ironically hopeful as children skipping and jumping or as immigrants going from *here* to *there.*

Everybody's Other World

Where am I?

New York City was my point of arrival in the United States. Even more accurately, New York City was the place where I realized that I was elsewhere, that I had left my familiar world, exchanging the dangers of political persecution for something tinged with uncertainty, hope, and the promise of discoveries that I might never share personally with those who remained behind. My enduring interest in how lives intertwine in the stories of Jewish and Latino writers was probably born in those early days, when fictional characters were my most reliable interlocutors, friends who did not look at me with puzzlement.

What does the United States mean when viewed with the special gaze of the foreigner, the recent or not so recent arrival who already feels a sense of belonging to an established culture? The position of such observers and participants in American society is somewhat detached: it elicits criticism, often through humor or denunciation, as it exhibits a desire to transform it by inflecting it with other dictions, inundating it with new rhythms and customs. The country is a spectacle, a kind of continuous show to be described with the amazement of one who knows that whatever happens in the States may be a clue to the future.

Tourists have their own way of reporting their finds. Such testimonies tend to explain the reason for undertaking the journey, justify its cost and distance, and express a renewed appreciation for home. But while a tourist's experience may be captured by souvenirs and other forms of the collector's detached curiosity, those who arrive with a one-way ticket have a different set of expectations. Senses are heightened; the new can be threatening and acquire an apocalyptic hold on the viewer. The trip with no return, particularly for those who have been persecuted and then saved by chance, offers very few possibilities for nostalgia. Nostalgia is the province of those who believe that their homeland is a welcoming place, somewhere to which they have a right. They hold a key that will eventually bring them back to a lost childhood and the safety of unspoken bonds. That feeling is shared by those who nourish a floating identity connected to an imaginary place of unproblematic belonging. *I am Italian, I am Greek, I am Cuban, I am Dominican*—that is often the refrain of people who may never have set foot in their alleged homelands. The peculiarities of life in the United States allow and even encourage these feelings of membership in societies far away, despite the geographical conditions of one's birth.

Polish Jews have a distinct place in this gallery of one-way ticket holders because they do not have the cushion of nostalgia for a place that massacred the vast majority of its Jews. What are they to long for? From what vantage point are they to look at things in a country whose language many did not know upon their arrival? Writing about the United States from within by nostalgics, outcasts, survivors, and would-be aristocrats reveals to us the instability of the country as reference, the ungraspable quality it has had as a grounding for individual experiences.

Isaac Bashevis Singer's characters live out their lives attempting to reach an agreement with the idea they have of their own destinies. Brought to the city by the sheer luck of the survivor, they speak to each other in Yiddish, English, Polish, and Russian. In the book *Shadows on the Hudson*, serialized in the Jewish newspaper *The Forward* in the 1950s, we encounter a gallery of just such characters, who are struggling to find meaning amid personal betrayals. One is Stanislaw Luria, who, abandoned by his wife, decides to take his life. In an attempt to discuss the measure, however, he visits Professor Shrage, a man he had met in Warsaw and who, like him, belonged to a moneyed and learned circle in that city. Now in New York, a bond seems to persist. Luria apologizes for not having announced his visit, saying that he telephoned but that he knows the professor avoids using the phone. The reply: "Avoid? I can't cope with it. The callers speak English, and it's difficult for me to make out what they're saying. I learned English from Shakespeare, but here they speak English so fast and it's all slang."[1] Rather than acknowledging a shortcoming in his own education, the professor charges New Yorkers with speaking the wrong kind of English.

In spite of the professor's admonishment against suicide, Luria persists in his decision: "Here, Professor, I find it tedious. I have nothing more to do. I have, so to speak, wrapped up all my business. As Shakespeare says, 'He that dies pays all debts.'"[2] Luria is a desperate man. His first wife and children were murdered by the Nazis, and Anna, whom he married in the States, has left him. The otherworldly Professor Shrage has no power of persuasion over him, but Shakespeare constitutes a sure bond between them. They may not speak English well, but they can quote Shakespeare to each other and mean what they say.

As for life in the United States, the understanding of what drives it is variable. To an angry Stanislaw Luria explaining the betrayal of his wife, it's money: "She's going to a man who deals in stocks on Wall Street. . . . She's become an American. There's only one love here—love for the dollar."[3] Anna herself, though tottering between love affairs, refuses to partake in the pessimism of those around her; instead, her failures open the door for bittersweet success: "This is America, not Europe! Anna told herself. Here one has to shake a leg and do things, not wander about with one's head in the clouds. Since the whole of America was predicated on achieving success, one had to be a success oneself."[4] And a success she becomes, a slender, elegant businesswoman who, though capable of saving her father's fortune, is nonetheless incapable of settling down with a man.

One certainty about life in the United States might be the dollar, but for Anna, the key to understanding the world that it creates lies in Freud. As she drives down Fifth Avenue she glances at store windows. "There was no end to the costly goods on display—clothes, jewelry, lingerie, furniture, silver—all the latest styles. Even the dust jackets of the new books seemed to be more colourful this year than ever before. There were thousands of talented people in New York who kept devising new charms, new variations, new attractions to entice customers, in exactly the same way as flowers decked themselves out in every imaginable color to attract the bees that pollinated them. Yes, Freud was right—everything was sex."[5]

What is New York? How to understand it as a place for conducting one's life? The characters in Singer's fiction wander the city. Stockbrokers, professors, theosophists, actors, swindlers, holy men and women, pretenders, and pathological truth-sayers all navigate a space shaped by their faithfulness to what was left behind and a sense of their new environment. The New York that serves as a backdrop to their discussions and travails varies with their mood like an ever-changing kaleidoscope. Each time they try to define the city, they find another version of their own circumstances. New York is a mirage, and when the allure of the new wears thin, they find a familiar underside. As Stanislaw Luria looks out the window of the el-train he considers the pawnshops, scrap-metal dealers selling their wares, and the mediocre eateries along the way. People entering the train reflect the bleakness of their surroundings:

How shabby they all looked! Raw faces, rough-hewn as
though with an ax, wild-eyed, outsized hands and feet. One
woman heaved herself in, so fat that she could barely squeeze
through the doorway. Her angry glance seemed to say: I'm
not fat for fun! When she sat down she occupied two seats.
And look at the clothes. Where did these people find such
garments? Their outlandish blouses and jackets the color of
sulphur, with clashing stripes and checks, reminded Luria of
Polish peasants and their *ciuchy*, the second-hand clothes they
used to sell in Targówek. Here poverty, ugliness, tasteless-
ness seemed to have crowded together. These people had no
scruples either: give them power and they would do exactly
what had been done in Russia. Each of them gave Luria
a single glance, then averted his eyes. Where did they live?
Where were they going? He would not have been surprised
if this EL was headed for Kowicz or Nizhni-Novgorod.[6]

Feeling that New York is Poland or Russia is not at all
sheltering. On the contrary, for Luria it is a proof of his
ongoing torment. Unable to leave, he is inextricably tied to
the grotesque. America becomes part of a bad joke played
against his hope of taking distance from his past.

Isaac Bashevis Singer's characters are, or wish to become,
travelers. Sometimes, as in *The Certificate*, their lives are domi-
nated by the administrative maneuvers needed to ensure a
departure from Europe that may save their lives.[7] Other
works of fiction by him dealing with life in America become
examples of a different desire to leave, tinged with a will to
commit suicide or find hope in a trip. *Shadows on the Hudson*
envisions the ultimate geographical escape as Florida. Two

characters who had experienced a youthful passion while in Poland now find themselves leaving their mates to enjoy an adulterous affair among palm trees and ocean views. The thrill of foreignness greets them in Florida—the warm air, blue sky; for a brief moment they seem to be experiencing a renewal. Perhaps America is emerging here, the optimism of a new life now linked to an exuberant New World landscape. Soon enough, however, real estate speculators, gossipy New Yorkers, and fellow Polish and Russian survivors emerge to convince the couple that the chance to make a change is but a dream. For them, the New World masquerades as the old. Florida's distance from New York is an illusion.

The United States is a place where Singer sees Jews as grotesque because they are disconcerted, scattered, and hopeless. Scholars grapple with thoughts that do not help them organize their lives, ordinary people crisscross in exchanges that frequently lead them to betray their friends and spouses, and holy men and women, though admired and respected, represent an almost impossible ideal. Without nostalgia, some search for their roots in familiar surroundings, such as the hopeless character who returns to Poland from Argentina in *Scum,* or the man who in Poland falls in love with dim-witted Shosha in an attempt to regain his lost religiosity.[8]

The American fictions of Isaac Bashevis Singer pose the need to escape because of embarrassment and lack of purpose. The survivors' European communities, now lost, provided a unity, a background against which talk about Freud, parapsychology, philosophy, art, and the practice of religion created a fundamental cohesiveness. In the United States, the unknown territory appears to be the old but without its glue. The characters, exposed as though on stage, perform their actions with an uncanny repetition that causes them shame and a desire to flee. But where to go?

Some, like Grein in *Shadows on the Hudson*, choose religion. He practices so rigorously that, in a successful bid out of the present, his appearance changes to resemble his own father's. Others look to Israel for salvation, as in the novel *Meshugah*.[9] There, after becoming entwined in a tangle of love affairs and pitiful rivalries featuring, as is frequently the case in Bashevis Singer, an attractive and unscrupulous stockbroker, the characters assemble in Fellini-like fashion for a trip that will no doubt only bring further aimlessness.

The ghost of an elusive America permeates Singer's work. Ungraspable and yet enveloping, this yearning is fed by an angry dissatisfaction with Europe. The problem with America, apparently, is that it cannot differentiate itself completely from the Old World. Where are these characters to look for America? They find it in the streets, in trains and restaurants, in the clothes that people wear, in a particular use of English. America is consumerism. Its contagious nature shapes newcomers and turns them into absurd, disheveled caricatures of what they should have been. New York and Miami, for their part, are names for the scattering of Jewish culture, places where the nakedness of secular Jewish life is exposed, condemned, and celebrated. The streets of New York are seen alternately as the dreaded stage for the destruction of European Jewry and as the key to an encompassing but unexplainable newness. Everything in Singer's United States is New York, even Florida, because New York is the web in which individual destinies are entangled and their possibility of becoming a community is dispersed. "No, Grein did not really understand America. He complained at every opportunity that American minds functioned according to categories different from those that operated in Europe, that people here were the biological antitheses of Europeans. Nonetheless Americanness had entered his bones."[10]

Life as a screenplay

Polish and Russian accents, Hebrew prayers, conversations in Yiddish and broken English that take place in coffee shops, apartments, and cars are transformed in the work of Oscar Hijuelos. We are still in New York, but to be certain of it we must turn on the television and watch. His novel *The Mambo Kings Sing Songs of Love* opens with an evocation of *I Love Lucy* and the energy that the Desi Arnaz character infuses in a group of New York Cubans. The dark-haired entertainer with a heavy Spanish accent who is married to Lucille Ball makes some cringe. His presence on TV grants him visibility as a stereotype, makes him into a joke at times, but invariably tells his story through a diction that encapsulates travel, distance. He is at home in the States, smiling, aggressively foreign, unfailingly intense. The television screen has been redefined as an entrance to the mainstream and, grounded in comical situations of the everyday, generates the same charge that Hollywood movies have elicited for generations of Latin American viewers. No doubt about it: Desi is a clown, his lines punctuated by canned laughter; but then, so is his wife, Lucille. Together, the dim-witted all-American cream puff of a housewife and her Cuban musician husband stand for a certain kind of good-natured situational humor that owes much to Desi's recent arrival in the United States.

The emergence of a Hispanic literature written in English within the United States produces in some the same kind of unease as Desi does: How to react to an English so textured with Spanish phrases and rhythms? And no less important: What to say about the easing of the Spanish language into English prose? These are questions of authenticity, about cohesion of literary traditions and the nature of the interpretive communities created by art and literature. Nobody here misses the language of Shakespeare. Characters understand one another, and when they cannot find the right English word, Spanish comes to the rescue.

Oscar Hijuelos is part of a generation of writers working in this highly textured language. He is a Hispanic from New York, the son of a Cuban family that emigrated in 1951. Hijuelos writes in his native English, creating an oblique relationship to the vibrant cultural and literary tradition of the island. The world of *The Mambo Kings* invites us to find Cuba again in traces of American popular culture.

The back and forth between Anglo-American and Hispanic cultures contains the equivalent of a third language, embedded in English and Spanish, in Junot Díaz's *The Brief Wondrous Life of Oscar Wao.*[11] Here, nerdy Oscar Wao finds an identity playing video games, as though the universal language of the screen will help him out of his miserable loneliness. The novel tells us, though, that the only way to understand his circumstances is through his Dominican past. By constructing the narrative in a manner reminiscent of Latin American historical fiction, Díaz suggests that his Dominican American characters are the product of the crisscrossing burdens they have carried since their arrival in the United States. Oscar Wao's video games evoke the impossibility of truly going from here to there and leaving everything behind. The violence of Dominican history cannot be erased by mere geographical displacement. In a world that turns claustrophobic, any departure only brings characters closer to their point of origin, whether implied or real.

The dismantling threat of caricature present in the frighteningly wide-eyed and energetic Carmen Miranda, with her towering hats and hyperrealistic gestures, and in Desi's accented speech is deemed to be a thing of the past by one of the characters in Hijuelos's *Mambo Kings,* who remembers it having been an honor, a kind of certificate of belonging, to have appeared on the *I Love Lucy* show. It represented the kind of collective passport that granted the most heightened form of reality: the tube, being watched, being broadcast. "When I heard the opening strains of the *I Love Lucy* show I got excited because I knew she was referring to an item of eternity, that episode in which my dead father and my uncle Cesar had appeared playing Ricky Ricardo's singing cousins fresh off the farm in Oriente Province, Cuba, and north in New York for an engagement at Ricky's night club, the Tropicana."[12] The novel's story of the two brothers, their love travails and involvement with music, is told in an easy-flowing language that highlights the sensual aspects of their lives. Food, lovemaking, betrayals, and everyday chatter are set against an effective musical background. The golden era of the past is represented both by the cohesion of the immigrant family in New York and the excellence of the Cuban musical tradition. All that was left behind, as well as all that was carried in the suitcases of the new arrivals, is encapsulated in the episodes of *I Love Lucy*. Ricky Ricardo is a key to the naturalization of Hispanic vocabulary and diction within English. Having been part of that, having appeared in the show, for these characters justifies their lives.

Spanish words appear in English without feeling foreign: "Nene—his uncle called out to him, and Eugenio charged down the hall. When Cesar lifted him up, Eugenio's feelings of emptiness went away"; and later: "*Oyeme, hombre,* he said, straightening Nestor's bow tie. 'Be strong. It'll be great. Don't be nervous, just do as we did during the rehearsals with Mr. Arnaz.'"[13] These are characters who live out their lives unhampered by language differences; they say what they mean in whatever way best serves their immediate needs. The apparent lack of preoccupation about style in language develops into a style of its own. Hijuelos has captured a way of speaking; it is not fractured, despite the inclusion of non-English words within the English, because Spanish does not function as an importation. It is a crucial medium for rendering a peculiar kind of experience. But what is this experience?

In *Mambo Kings*, books and words have nearly disappeared as subjects of the narrative; neither Shakespeare nor Cervantes are evoked as a model of communication. Life is identified instead with popular culture, television, and, in particular, popular music. *The Mambo Kings* locates itself in a terrain of sheer intuition and pleasure. All we need to do is forget what language we are reading and enjoy the unproblematic spectacle.

Hispanic American writers like Hijuelos, Díaz, and Cristina García, author of *Dreaming in Cuban*, are creating a language that wants to undo the differences between English and Spanish. "I met Max at a downtown basement club a few months ago," Pilar, a character in *Dreaming in Cuban*, explains. "He came over and started speaking to me in Spanish (his mother is Mexican) as if he'd known me for years. I liked him right away. When I brought him around to meet my parents, Mom took one look at his beaded headband and the braid down his back and said, *'Sácalo de aquí.'* When I told her that Max spoke Spanish, she simply repeated what she said in English: 'Take him away.'"[14]

This kind of writing at its best is removed from the merely picturesque and addresses itself to a community of readers that does not see being Hispanic as a pretext for situational humor or public introspection. Television and popular music played and continue to play an important role in the naturalization of Hispanic intellectuals as a cultural group both separate from and integrated within the mainstream of the United States, redefining the terms in which we think of writing in English and Spanish. Phrases in Spanish referring to food, parts of the body, nicknames, and insults become part of the new sound of English in a writing that is openly colloquial and rooted in everyday reality. This writing, these television shows, these musical sounds, we are told, reflect the present situation of the country. Desi, the newcomer of the past, has now defined a norm, and may be despised as a demeaned incarnation of the terminally *simpático* Hispanic.

For Lourdes in *Dreaming in Cuban*, her Brooklyn neighborhood grants an occasion for pondering the relationship with people from different places, converging in the spectacle of the city. She wonders: "What happens to their languages? The warm burials they leave behind? What to their passions lying stiff and untranslated in their breasts?"[15] Far from embracing an optimistic cosmopolitanism or a nostalgic Cuban patriotism, Lourdes feels herself to be wholly in the United States. But the United States evoked here is made up of the patchwork of languages and unfinished business brought by those she sees in the street. The very meaning of being in New York is sustained by her uncertainty about the layers that make up the city.

What happens to these people's languages? Works such as García's and Hijuelos's suggest a solution. No longer concerned with picturesque representations of Hispanics, they present Spanish as part of normal, everyday English diction. Isaac Bashevis Singer's Professor Shrage walked the same streets and, feeling that Shakespeare was on his side, posited the radical foreignness of English to itself: The problem with Americans is that they speak slang; let's keep languages distinct. Paradoxically, Singer's Yiddish-speaking characters have a purist relationship with their sense of who they are. It is an allegiance to a certain quality of connections among individuals inextricably linked together by history and hesitant to define their bond when it strays from religious practice.

Beyond the national: Let's watch together

If for many New York epitomizes the United States, for others Hollywood provides the framework for rethinking not only the Americas but the world more generally.

Guillermo Cabrera Infante, a Cuban émigré widely acclaimed as one of the great innovators of Latin American fiction and an outspoken enemy of Castro, relocated to Europe in 1965, first to Madrid and later to London. His writing, characterized by parody and punning, is wed to the musical rhythms of Latin America and the images of Hollywood. Cabrera Infante was fascinated by performance and created for himself a dramatic presence enhanced by dark humor and often startling associations. When I met him, I was struck by his kinship with Manuel Puig, the Argentine novelist best known for the novel *The Kiss of the Spider Woman*, who spent most of his life in Europe, New York, and Brazil. Both turned every conversation into an invitation to perform a role. Exile probably intensified this aspect of their personalities, transforming Cabrera Infante into an extreme version of a Cuban character, and Manuel Puig into the mannered embodiment of a small-town Argentinean thrown almost by surprise into the larger world.

Cabrera Infante's best known work, the novel *Tres tristes tigres* (Three trapped tigers), features Havana night life and is a testimony to his love for bolero, its vocalists and its lyrics. Similarly, Manuel Puig's fascination with tango, movies, and local Argentine diction shapes his fiction with the peculiar longing for the original grounding place felt by those who live far from their homeland.

Cabrera Infante and Puig are the two most salient representatives of a certain vision of the United States as provider of the ultimate machine of interpretation: film. In a series of lectures devoted to movies, gathered in the 1979 volume *Arcadia todas las noches* (Arcadia every night), Cabrera Infante maintains that film fulfills the function once accorded to myth. For him, the great directors of the American screen, above all Orson Welles, John Huston, Howard Hawkes, and Alfred Hitchcock, provide a system of interpretation for reality itself, making powerful cultural interventions through their use of the camera and perspective on storytelling. His admiration for these artists is carried over to the way in which Cabrera Infante conceives of his fictions, framing characters and structuring scenes that privilege the visual and musical aspects of writing. American film has given Cabrera Infante a language and a vision.

Yet—how well does he actually understand these movies? In a humorously shocking revelation for a man who purported to be a great expert on film, he says that the famous 1938 radio broadcast by Orson Welles, *The War of the Worlds,* whose staged Martian invasion sent people into a full-blown panic, would not have frightened him had he been living in New Jersey at the time. The reason? He did not know English. This fact, however, did not in any way diminish the genealogy into which he inscribed himself, for images and sounds acquire transnational meaning as they become an exile's refuge. No need to know English to understand what is at stake.

Film is itself a language, the great matrix of contemporary culture. But what kind of understanding does it provide?

Two men sitting in a cell in the 1970s—Molina, a gay man convicted of corrupting minors, and Arregui, a left-wing revolutionary—suggest one response to this question. Both are characters in Manuel Puig's *The Kiss of the Spider Woman.* Molina tells movies to Arregui almost non-stop. The context is that Molina has been planted in the cell by the police to induce Arregui to betray names and activities that would allow them to kill or incarcerate members of his political group. The novel describes—through dialogue, police reports, and other materials—how the logic of the films being told creates a relationship between the two men that exceeds both the parameters planned by the state and the men's attraction toward each other.

Entangled in one of the plots that Molina has been tell-

ing, about a conflict of political will in which an allegedly
suffering diva falls passionately in love with a Nazi, Arregui
appears to return the love that Molina feels for him and
trusts him with delivering a message to his comrades once
he is freed from prison. The novel closes with Molina being
shot in the street while Arregui is tortured by the police.

Flirting with the way life imitates film, Puig gives us the
heightened emotions of melodrama as a phenomenon of
contagion as Molina dies for the man he loves.

Film acts here as a system of translation that blurs
national and political interests in favor of heightened emotions. How can we be both outside and inside a conflict?
How radical can our internal exile become in the face of
retold film scenes? *The Kiss of the Spider Woman* renders a vision
of total participation in a national reality that becomes
something else entirely when it is reinterpreted by film.
The *here* and *there* of the characters is resolved through death
(Molina's) and torture (Arregui's), suggesting that the
detachments of exile fostered by Hollywood are frequently
a mirage.

Many of Puig's characters strive to speak the language
of the movies: little old ladies who mind their neighbors'
business, as in *Cae la noche tropical* (*Tropical Night Falling*, 1988),
boys who describe movies to their friends in small provincial towns, as in *La traición de Rita Hayworth* (*Betrayed by
Rita Hayworth*, 1968) and housewives who listen to boleros
and tangos, as in *Boquitas pintadas* (*Heartbreak Tango*, 1969). If
women's hearts are broken by the death of the undeserving
Don Juan of *Heartbreak Tango*, it is not because of the raw

attractiveness of the semi-illiterate young man—who, as his obituary states at the outset of the novel, was to be commended mainly for his *simpatía*, personal charm; rather, it is because of the women's power to locate him in the context of the music and films that shape their lives. Only then do their experiences acquire the prestige of belonging to a tradition, thus becoming much more than trivial anecdotes.

Heartbreak Tango provides the equivalent of a musical score, through epigraphs that quote tango lyrics and a suggestive array of film images that determine the very look of the characters. More than fiction influenced by film, Puig offers fiction *as* film, playing against genre definition. This capacity to shape life is what Cabrera Infante wants to convey when he says that film is the great myth of our time.

In this view, Hollywood is not as much a producer of illusions as the provider of a framework for inflecting experience and granting meaning to daily chatter. So strong is the influence of film that even local literary tradition becomes redefined by the magnetism exercised by movie stars. In a witty and humorous obituary for Manuel Puig, Guillermo Cabrera Infante described how Puig had once given him a much-cherished present, a list of leading Latin American writers re-identified as female movie stars: "Borges, blind, was cross-eyed Norma Shearer. Commentary: 'Oh, how dignified.' Carpentier was Joan Crawford: 'Oh, how fierce.' Asturias was Greta Garbo: 'Only for that gift of the Nobel.' Juan Rulfo was Greer Garson; Cortázar was Hedy Lamarr: 'So cold and remote'; Lezama was, surprise! Lana Turner, and Vivien Leigh, 'so sick and temperamental,' was

Sábato. Vargas Llosa was Esther Williams, 'so disciplined,' and Carlos Fuentes was Ava Gardner, who had an aura of glamour, though Puig wondered, 'But, can she act?' García Márquez was Elizabeth Taylor: 'Beautiful face, awful body.'"[16]

The language of Shakespeare? Cervantes? The great innovators of the Spanish language, those writers whose linguistic creativity has prompted many a critic to say that there have truly been only two great periods of literature in Spanish—the Golden Age (Early Modern) and the twentieth century—must be translated to be properly understood. And the translation is not into English, or French, or any other written language, but into the visual. Pictures of movie stars, as though we were watching a silent movie, have the eloquence to transmit what's needed: instant recognition, integration into the all-embracing mythmaking of film.

The lives of Puig's, Hijuelos's, and García's characters and the references in Cabrera Infante's obituary rest on the assumption of a virtual homeland, a community of imaginary lives and heightened passions that exists beyond nationality and, as a result, is profoundly intimate. U.S. culture is perceived as though it came from nowhere—or as though it could come from anywhere. Shot through with nostalgia and humor, the use of Hispanicized English in novels such as *Dreaming in Cuban*, *The Mambo Kings*, and *The Brief Wondrous Life of Oscar Wao* suggests that the resolution of longing does not lie in the past but in the forging of a literature that gives voice to an in-betweenness, a neither here nor there.

Considering the United States from both within and without, these writers agree: the place is a mirage constructed by those willing to invest their destinies in its exploration. Its hook for the imagination may very well lie in the lack of urgency with which it poses questions about its own cultural identity.

Who Is the Woman of the Mother Tongue?

The mother tongue

The mother tongue is the one spoken to us by our mothers, anchored in the assurance of a nurturing body and grounding our first experiences in the world. In that sense, it precedes the moment of doubt, the detachment implied in irony and criticism. Myths about female abnegation, maternal selflessness, and unconditional acceptance nourish beliefs in an original moment when language and things have a transparent relationship.

On the other side of the spectrum, Medeas, witches, treacherous sirens, and manipulative enchantresses represent the monstrous exception, a cruelty that leaves us speechless and fascinated with the same enduring emotion as its hyperbolically positive counterpart.

Motherly love and exile

There is no doubt about the grounding power of motherhood in the popular imagination. We are told that having only one mother and one birthplace makes our nationality and the language that we learn from her identical and inter-dependent. From that perspective, the truth about our roots requires unconditional love. Mothers are the link with the homeland, and if the chain is unbroken, the mother-child pair becomes the opposite of exile.

But what if we were to encounter neither of these extremes? What if the answer to our questions about self-recognition was best evoked by the engulfing movement of quicksand or the fleeting lucidity of a fainting spell?

Apathy, distance, absent-mindedness, and abandonment are also ways of conceiving motherhood. Clarice Lispector, Jean Rhys, Nathalie Sarraute, and Marguerite Duras are among a few writers who have delineated a sense of exile stemming from those fractures. In this view, exile becomes an originary condition, and love conveys the distress of implied rejection.

The surrealist artist Giorgio de Chirico recognized the otherworldliness of the Brazilian writer Clarice Lispector and painted her portrait; Caetano Veloso, a Brazilian musician with the capacity to assimilate and transform words and sounds, considered her an inspiration; and the French author Hélène Cixous expressed admiration for Lispector in her writing.

Clarice Lispector was born in the Ukraine of Jewish parents in 1920. She was, however, a child conceived in the spirit of immigration—when she was only two months old, her family left their war-ravaged homeland for Brazil—and her life was marked by residence in various European and U.S.

cities.[1] Although she wrote in several genres—indeed, she regarded the very idea of genre unnecessarily limiting—it is in her short stories that the full impact of her ironic gaze is to be discerned. Perhaps the fact that her mother died when she was nine years old contributed to the freedom of her writing, where facts and emotions are sustained on the lightest and most fragile of platforms. As with the francophone Russian writer Nathalie Sarraute, French writer Marguerite Duras, and Dominican-born Jean Rhys, her language has the familiarity of the everyday while becoming, at times, abrupt, as though foreignness and familiarity were inextricably intertwined.

Lispector is at her best when writing about intimate situations: an old woman's birthday as she forgets and is forgotten by her family; the petty crime of an elderly math professor; evanescent encounters that lead to nothing.

Love and pregnancy

A pregnant woman and a French explorer meet in the depths of Africa, exchange gazes, are portrayed in magazines. She is the smallest woman in the whole world; he has found a subject of study. We are told that she loves him. Yet the line that separates explorer and woman is unstable. The protagonists of Clarice Lispector's "The Smallest Woman in the World" could not be more different from one another, and she loves him precisely because of that difference. "In the humidity of the jungle, there do not exist these cruel refinements; love is not to be devoured, love is to find boots pretty, love is to like the strange color of a man who is not black, love is to smile out of love at a ring that shines."[2]

For Little Flower—the woman—love is based in the details offered to her gaze: a ring, boots, his skin color. A language soon develops between her and the explorer. We do not know what the explorer feels, but we are told that his compulsive note-taking during their attempts at conversation masks an acute shyness. Romance ensues with the intimation that she remains an object of curiosity for him.

Beyond the class or cultural differences evoked in certain versions of Pygmalion, what is at stake here is the very meaning of love. In the modern and contemporary Pygmalion tradition, the interest resides in the conflicts of overcoming differences. Is it good to access a higher realm of culture and consumption? Does it elevate either of the individuals in the couple? Typically, the one to be educated, bettered, saved from vulgarity and instincts, is the woman. Yet, another type of romance, exemplified by Josef von Sternberg's 1930 film *Blue Angel*, stresses the negative possibilities of the blurring of differences by presenting an older male as he heads ineluctably toward damnation, blind to the gap that separates him from a young seductress. The implication, perhaps, is that men should be more reluctant to deny their identity than women, who have a greater chance of improving themselves through love.[3] Women, are seen as finding themselves, while men lose themselves, victims of their own passions and of female manipulation.

Lispector's story is a rejection of the conventional take

on cultural clashes and love. Little Flower's love is nothing short of materialistic because, we are told, she loves to possess. The explorer, for his part, cannot utter what he feels. And yet the tale closes with an anonymous old woman, who, upon reading about the existence of Little Flower in the newspaper, comments: "It just goes to show. I'll say one thing though—God knows what He's about."[4]

What has the old woman understood?[5] The cliché "God knows," accompanied by "what He's about" points toward a shared secret, a sense of belonging to a group that has the key for understanding the meaning of this unusual encounter. On the other side stand the newspaper readers, consumers of difference, who rejoice in their sameness as they consider the enigma of explorer and minute woman. For them, Little Flower is a native par excellence: naive and yet materialistic, taken in by superficial appearances. Consumption of foreign goods, exoticism, and fear of the unknown are blended in her representation, and her diminutive size is such that she may be confused with folkloric ornaments and cute airport souvenirs from faraway lands. The fact that she is pregnant only emphasizes the threat of change posed by natives: they will multiply; the future will be theirs if others do not watch out.

Yet Little Flower is bound by love. There is something almost brutal in the acknowledgment that what she experiences is love because of the unsentimental treatment of the situation, which makes love into something we are barely able to qualify, a shorthand for something we are meant to know but do not recognize here. It is as though in telling us too much about Little Flower's emotions, the very possibility of representing feelings had been snatched away.

The unblinking curiosity, and bewilderment, about the quality of love is again Lispector's subject in the story "The Chicken." In it, a bird singled out to become dinner lays an egg, which the children of the house interpret as a sign that it loves them. The same bewilderment in the use of the term as in "The Smallest Woman in the World" is present here.

Less blatant than the chicken, the mother in "The Smallest Woman in the World," Little Flower, offers her sentiment in the language of the reader, which makes her seem less different. She is pregnant and she is capable of love. What is the explorer to do? The story does not tell us whether they stayed together or fell apart, whether his notes were valuable, or what, if anything, in her caused him to leave or stay. We suspect that neither of them changed, that the encounter was brief and that the rifts between the scientific realm and human experience are resolved without sentimentality.

The final appeal to God's mysterious ways restates a silent pact between the pair. Like the bond between children and bird in "The Chicken," which allows the kids to drift away after having obtained a pardon for the chicken, this couple is already fading into the background. The intensity of their encounter is as fleeting as the domestic drama in "The Chicken." "Mummy! Mummy! Don't kill the chicken; she's laid an egg! The chicken loves us!" say the children. Yet the mother is not about to be swept away, either by the enthusiasm of her children or by the sentimentalism of her husband, who feels guilty for having made the chicken run, not knowing that she was pregnant. Rather, "the mother, feeling weary, shrugged her shoulders." Not unlike the old woman in "The Smallest Woman in the World," she knows that although life may be mysterious, there is nothing to get excited about when an egg is laid. The chicken itself (or rather, as the story says, *herself*) is not granted permanent human traits because, "in flight or in repose, when she gave birth or while pecking grain, hers was a chicken's head, identical to that drawn at the beginning of time. Until one day they killed her and ate her."[6]

What are these stories telling us about motherhood and love? With sharp-edged humor, Lispector rejects common-place treatments of the subject.[7] The chicken and Little Flower are two extreme representations of mothers, but in her view, their identity as such is not to be enshrined. The chicken's reprieve from death does not last long, and Little Flower gains no depth for being pregnant, while the children's mother in "The Chicken," in her weariness, seems to negate the idea that mothers are deserving of any special status.

The chicken was a beneficiary of the husband's and the children's pity; the mother remains indifferent, as though the feast of sentiment and sympathy is not part of her nature. Little Flower is happier; she is in love. Her love, however, runs counter to common sense: it is a celebration of her capacity not to be subsumed by her feelings. Lispector, in depicting pregnancy and motherhood, avoids equating females with excess, and motherhood with unequivocal nurturing.

An entry in Witold Gombrowicz's diary describes a female friend's reaction to the painful agony of a dog: "She suddenly changed into a female—she took refuge in her sex . . . what a sudden eruption of gender into the realm of pain; as if gender could cope somehow with the pain. . . . She became a female, that is love, that is pity. She bent over the dog with a mother's tenderness. Is it possible that as a female she could do no more than as a human being? Or, did she retreat into her sex in order to escape her own humanity?"[8] For Gombrowicz, the specificity of gender debases what is universally human; he is thus inclined to disregard what he considers to be the most feminine of reactions: love and pity. In this particular situation, the woman's pity has the cruel result of prolonging the dog's agony. Misplaced, female sympathy is destructive both of its beneficiaries and of the one bestowing it, since it makes the woman into a mere exponent of her own gender.

Lispector's carefully drawn apathetic female characters in marked contrast to the protagonists of the stories she authored under a self-defined erotic rubric[9] try to avoid the softness of femininity, and so experience their own humanity as a question mark. Bird and woman in "The Chicken" share their separation from the family. The chicken, we are told, is just what she seems: a chicken; and the woman, recognizing that fact, does not place a particular value on the egg as a symbol of motherhood.

But children need an uplifting tale of motherhood; they want to believe that their emergence into the world is meaningful. They need to protect the pregnant chicken and forget it quickly. They would like to think that Little Flower, instead of loving the boots and ring of the strange explorer, is wholly engrossed by her future delivery. If that were not the case, a most important bond would be severed. It would not be possible to go back home; an origin and point of departure would be lost. Motherhood, home, and love belong together as an origin; substituting it for exile creates a wound too intense to bear.

The dizziness and aimlessness of the female characters in Lispector's *Family Ties* suggest that being born and giving birth are part of a neutral continuum to be portrayed in a measured, unsentimental manner. Rather than giving rise to language, mothers are immutable and cryptic; their silence is sometimes enabling and, at other times, a road map to a dead end.

Where is she in this picture?

Marguerite Duras was born in 1914 in French Indochina, where she spent her younger years and had formative experiences. In her writing she went back time and again to those places and people she knew, with the peculiar spirit of recollection belonging to someone who does not quite believe that her life can be told in a conventional manner. Rather than organizing her facts linearly, she opted to evoke her experiences as scenes. Her writing, and the films made from her works, eloquently pose questions about silence, sexual pleasure, and love.

At the time of her death in Paris in 1996, she was considered a major French literary figure, yet one who had not forgotten that she was an outsider, a woman born elsewhere. Not only had she not forgotten it, but most of her work turns around the capacities of an observer who is, at the same time, a protagonist in events.

Duras's characters search for meaning in a manner that is often futile and obsessive. Such is the case in *The Ravishing of Lol Stein* (1964), in which a woman tries to figure out, by spying on a particular set of people over time, the nature of a humiliation she suffered in her past. Although the enigma might be unraveled by looking at the characters themselves as they interact in a scene, Duras proposes that contemplating people as if they were in a photograph might better reveal the meaning of their lives.

The Lover contains autobiographical materials concerning the erotic relationship of a young woman and an older lover in Indochina. The book invites us to *see* rather than reflect. The insistence on the present tense brings us straight into individual scenes, and the straightforward language in which they are depicted builds the illusion that we are being addressed directly. The young Duras's attachment to the Chinese lover reminds us of Lispector's Little Flower, for whom loving meant an attachment to material details, but in spite of the title, this is more a portrait of Duras than of her lover.

What are we told? First, we learn about a face. It belongs to the author. She quotes a man who, when she is already old, tells her: "I've known you for years. Everyone says you were beautiful when you were young, but I want to tell you I think that you are more beautiful now than then. Rather than your face as a young woman, I prefer your face as it is now. Ravaged."[10]

We are reading, then, the testimony of a beautiful woman. The author/narrator agrees with this witness: her face has not lost its contours; age has made it become a reflection of what she really is. She assures us that she likes it now better than when she was younger.

The Lover is a book in which faces tell how time has unfolded and is being lived. Youth, in this perspective, is a distraction from what matters: the identity of the bearer of the face.

Duras became a heavy drinker in her mature years, and she claims that one could already discern the alcoholism in her young face. Even though the novel's title ostensibly points to a love affair and the beginning concerns Duras's face, what interests her is another woman's face: that of her mother.

After Duras's father died, her mother decided to stay with her three children in Vietnam, where she was a schoolteacher, rather than return to France. The experience of being white people of modest means in the Vietnam of the time resonates with the life of Jean Rhys growing up in the West Indies. Cut off from both natives and colonialists, these were people who had no experience of being part of any mainstream.

Duras's mother liked to gauge her children's growth by having their pictures taken. She would then take the photographs home and compare them with other photos to ascertain whether they had become taller. In this regard, she was like the tourist in Elias Canetti's *Earwitness,* who could only truly see the places he had visited after he'd developed his pictures. Duras's mother had trouble being uncomplicatedly present and focusing, through personal observation, on her children's development. Indeed, she is portrayed in the novel as being profoundly distracted and unhappy, caught up in the web of an alternate reality. Duras, commenting on one of the photographs, reflects that she can tell from the way they were dressed that their mother had been in one of those states of mind that prevented her from attending to the details of their appearance.

Her mother's frequent mood swings, which took her from a state of generous exhilaration to one of utter dejection, remained a profound mystery for Duras. She asks herself whether it was an intuition about the impending death of her husband, problems in the marriage, or dissatisfaction with the children that clouded her life and theirs so much that even photographs could tell the mood of the moment. And it is those moods that constitute the main interest of the photographs for Duras: even when her mother appears in them directly, she manifests herself most intensely through her offspring.

The children bear the presence of the mother, the void that her sadness has imposed on them, the weight of her unforgiving detachment. And yet, we are told, she had lots of friends, was always surrounded by people; this was so, Duras says with the directness of denunciation, because of her intelligence and lively personality. One persona for the friends and another for the children, this mother presents

Duras's origin as a knot that may only be untied by looking closely at what she calls the "photograph of despair."

Why is the mother's despair so unbearable? Why not think about it in terms of her suffering rather than blame her for shortcomings in raising the children? Duras writes as though she were the implied counterpart of the narrator in Lispector's two stories. But whereas Lispector's is the voice of apathy, in Duras we listen to the shortchanged child who senses a secret that has not been told.

Was the mother's liveliness with non-family members an act? Who was this woman? A memory comes back with the answer: "I've never seen it before. Never seen my mother in the state of being mad. Which she was. From birth. In the blood. She wasn't ill with it, for her it was like health"[11]— meaning it was simply her way of being. The realization is not enough to exonerate her; she should have given more, been more open, less enigmatic. Rather than providing Duras with a language and a rich, straightforward way of referring to the world, her legacy is doubt and suspicion.

The mother is a black hole. She does not leave an inheritance in the form of words. Her way of seeing was through photographs, and Duras, faithful to her genealogy, describes herself from photographs as well. As she points out an idiosyncratic sadness in a picture, we recognize her kinship with her mother. That sadness, she is convinced, bears her name. Reality, she learned, is to be grasped at a distance, through the lens of a camera, and in this way the explicit tale of maternal indifference and rejection by her lover becomes acceptance of the mother's mode of understanding.

The novel's language is so intimate that it is difficult to distinguish fiction from autobiography. Once we know this, the evocation of the romance in *The Lover* confirms the photographic logic imposed from birth. Sex is a collection of scenes, the lover's presence recollected as though the affair were an assemblage of stills. Because nothing is a given, everything has to be explained and observed in detail. Away from the mother's sight, but possessing the same imperative to record and watch, Duras enters her first sexual liaison as a voyeur of her own life.

The mother's triumph has been imperceptibly achieved as a legacy of detachment. Evoking her means delving into something that makes the very experience of plenitude impossible. Uprooted and ill at ease both in Vietnam and in France, Duras's mother, in seeming to have always given less than enough, grants a peculiar eloquence to an art that has no particular trust in words.

A daughter as her mother's suitor

Nathalie Tcherniak, who became the writer Nathalie Sarraute after she took the name of her husband, was born in Ivanovo, Russia, in 1900 and died in Paris in 1990. Together with Michel Butor and Alain Robbe-Grillet she was an innovator of French narrative and founder of the *nouveau roman* movement. She came to France as a two-year-old with her mother after her parents' divorce, though as a child she traveled frequently to St. Petersburg and Geneva to stay with relatives. Fluent in French, Russian, and German, she became the kind of polyglot that was so admired in Jewish families such as her own.

Her writing interrogates the very notion of voice. When we open one of her novels we feel we have entered a room in which a conversation is already under way. We cannot take part until we understand the multiple layering of what is being said and how the words, given to us in whispers or in shrill, abrupt statements, function as part of a metaphoric chain. Although we may not be going forward, we know we are going deeper, as though we were traveling on a long, inward-turning spiral.

A language we think we understand perfectly well may still startle us. The words may be familiar, but their purpose, the way they normally take us to straightforward redundant meanings, is disconcertingly missing. It is that foreignness inside everyday speech that Sarraute works into her writings. Close to poetry, her fiction invites us to squint our eyes and sharpen our ears in order to better see and hear what surrounds us. Translation is necessary from one level of language to another, but secrets remain embedded, as though we could not reduce what is said to anything but its own repetition. Echoes, ironic puns, and a love of proliferation contribute to create a noise and rhythm that require the reader to act as interlocutor.

The 1983 publication of *Childhood* marked the first time that Sarraute's work became a mainstream success. Until then, though admired and recognized, she was known as a writer for an elite, literary audience. Despite her repeated assertions that she would not write an autobiography,

Childhood collects memories of her early years, which emerge in the course of a conversation between her and a double who is at times mocking, at others cooperative, but always eager to hear more.

The book is about her fascination with her mother, with whom she lived intermittently. Most of her life was spent with her father and stepmother, Vera; when a daughter was born from this union, Sarraute's position in the household became secondary.

Russian accents in French apartments, walks in the Luxembourg Gardens, gray places in France, and splendid recollections of St. Petersburg color remembrances that always prove unsatisfying. Vividness of memory is to be found not in the evocations of place but in the feelings elicited by viewing her indifferent mother: "Curiously enough that indifference, that casualness, were part of her charm, in the literal sense of the word, she charmed me. . . . No word, however powerfully uttered, has ever sunk into me with the same persuasive force as some of hers."[12]

Sarraute's mother disappears and appears in her life without warning. She leaves France for St. Petersburg precipitously, relegating Nathalie to a throwaway room in her father's apartment, the enduring trace of a failed relationship. The child feels like a guest in her father's home and perceives herself as abandoned. At the same time, the mother's travels back and forth between Paris and St. Petersburg are a source of wonder, for they allow her to remain in touch with an origin that Sarraute, who remembers nothing of her life in Russia, has forgotten.

When she is present, Sarraute's mother teaches little Nathalie that she, the mother, is the most beautiful of all creatures. Unconditional love and admiration are obligatory. The mother's indifference is part of her charm because, being so well loved, she exudes an elegance when she shrugs feelings off or acts distracted, as though she deserves to receive depth and intensity but is not obliged to give back in kind. The sense that the mother belongs to a natural aristocracy that entitles her to receive tribute brings turmoil to Sarraute as a child. In *Childhood*, Sarraute describes her embarrassment upon thinking that a doll she sees at the hairdresser's might be more beautiful than her mother. What if her mother is not so beautiful after all? What if she has the skin of a monkey, as she at times imagines? What kind of child is it that does not recognize unconditionally the superiority of her mother's appearance? Indifference, detachment, may be part of the mother's charm, but it is sinful for the child.

The tone Sarraute uses to sketch her mother is different from that of Marguerite Duras. While Duras speaks almost triumphantly about uncovering her mother's madness when she looks at a photograph, Sarraute recalls with guilt the moment when her admiration for her own mother shifts.

After an absence of more than two years, Sarraute's mother returns to Paris. The reunion between mother and child, now eleven, is to take place at the hotel where her mother is staying. Because she is old enough to get there by herself, Sarraute endures the experience alone. She recalls the streets that took her from Alésia to Porte d'Orléans in detail, as well as the name of the hotel, L'Idéal. Once she gets there, she has to ask for her by her new name, Madame Boretzki.

At first, her mother seems a stranger. She sports a new, unflattering hairdo similar to her stepmother Vera's, and she is a few pounds overweight. Still, Sarraute is happy to see her and the first impression is dispelled when she recognizes the familiar charm.

The ease with which her mother traverses cultural differences is an integral part of her powerful presence: "It sometimes happens at meals," Sarraute recalls, "that she forgets she is in France, and if she is speaking Russian and wants to say something that the maid serving at table isn't supposed to understand, she says it in French, and it is sometimes an uncomplimentary remark. Then Vera reminds her in Russian that she is in France, and she blushes and expresses her regret, in Russian this time. . . . Our meals are transformed by her presence."[13]

How wonderful to be able to navigate different languages so effortlessly and render one's mistakes into another attribute of one's elegance. Sarraute's mother's magnetism is such that she can turn language deficiencies into a source of personal exuberance. When Sarraute returns to the hotel to see her mother again, she learns that she has already left. A short while later, a card addressed to Vera arrives at the apartment. The message is clear: Sarraute's mother thanks Vera for having succeeded in turning her daughter into a complete egotist.

The language with which Sarraute relates this situation

does not imply abandonment. By then Sarraute has come to terms with living in Vera's household and even sees her in a more positive light. Instead, she feels humiliated. Not only does the mother not share her feelings, but she jilts her own child.

Of course, the daughter herself appears to break the bond on her own when she doubts the mother's beauty. Could she have loved more? What would have prevented the mother's return to St. Petersburg? Could the child have stopped the travel, anchored the mother so that she might become the source of words and perceptions, and of a warm, uncritical sense of belonging to a place?

Literature, the world of reading, gives Sarraute an alternative means for understanding her situation. It is not Russian or French but English that nourishes her, stories by Charles Dickens of the lives of orphans and poor children who experience the same loneliness that she feels.

Without sentimentality, the mother has delivered a message and the best revenge for the child turned rejected suitor emerges from pages in a language not covered in the maternal itineraries.

A woman from home

Visas and passports, mislaid hopes for change, permeate the literature of Isaac Bashevis Singer, from his earliest narratives to the posthumous *Meshugah.* I return to him here because, as in a spiral, his travels speak to the issues developed in this section.

In Singer's novel *Scum*, the main character, Max Barander, a Polish Jew who immigrated to Argentina in the early 1900s, has a problem: after the death of his only son, Max becomes impotent and his wife loses her interest in both sex and life. Max decides to go back to the place of his birth to see if he can find a solution to his problem.

Max made considerable money in Argentina, so his return to Poland does not entail the same sacrifices that other immigrants had to make to revisit their homeland. This trip is also different from most in the two purposes it serves: to mark his success as a businessman and to take him back to a source of energy that might rejuvenate him and restore his sexual potency. Singer draws Max in great detail, signaling his psychological capacity to become just about anything. His flexibility is not a virtue, however; he can lie, betray, and take advantage of others. His adaptability and opportunism go hand in hand in the Argentina he has inhabited since the place was turning into the prostitution center evoked by tango lyrics.

Max's impotence disappears once he arrives in Poland, but his sexuality, rather than being a celebration of regained youth, only reveals his lack of focus and unreliability as he gets entangled in unsavory affairs. A member of the cast of characters that readers of the Argentine author Roberto Arlt will recognize as marked by the kind of humiliation and moral skepticism of Buenos Aires and tango, Max toys with the different possibilities opened up for him in Poland.[14] Finally he reaches his goal, Krochmalna Street, where he goes into a tavern. Familiar smells, foods, and expressions greet him. But when he explains that he has come back to the place where he once lived, a bemused comment reminds him that nothing is really different: "When people come here they say it feels like home. Once a man from London showed up and drove over to Falenicz with us. In London, he said, there's no clean air—it's all smoke and the sun doesn't shine. Every day there's a fog and it rains, too. There money is weighed by the pound or the Devil knows what. But one thing is the same everywhere—you have to hand out bribes constantly."[15]

Max's trip is, to a certain extent, merely a geographic displacement. The same system of bribery is to be found in London, Poland, Argentina. The food may smell and taste different in Poland, things are certainly less modern, more provincial, but all places are similar in their lack of reliability. However, Max's voyage was not undertaken for the sake of finding purity; he wanted to recover his desire for women and ability to perform sexually. Once he accomplishes this, he is seemingly ready to go back. But where will he go?

Returning to Buenos Aires might masquerade as going back to *a* home. After all, it is where his wife lives, and he has real estate holdings there. Since Max did not seem to be looking for his origins, a round trip might be possible.

But Max's search has widened. Among his experiences in Poland are spiritualist séances, from which he emerges feeling alternately duped and inspired, and conversations in which he discusses the possibility of becoming a pimp in Buenos Aires by importing unsuspecting young women from Poland.[16] However, if the idea of being part of the white slave trade takes his own capacity for sleaze to new depths, his courtship of a rabbi's daughter, Tsirele, opens him up to an atmosphere of holiness.

In the novel, the observant Jewish home conveys the fascination of the exotic: the family is different, its members more austere, more direct, uninterested in money; above all, they have an air of wisdom, not just about Judaism but about life.

The rabbi's family represents one version of Jewish roots in Poland, and although their world is complete, it is not insulated from what goes on outside. Max is afraid that they will discover his contradictory layers and reject him: "The rebettzin mumbled something with her thin lips and made a sign that she could not speak. The sun reflected on her wig and lit up silken hairs of many hues. Max suddenly felt afraid of this woman. He sensed that even though she was observant and lived in a religious world, she thoroughly understood all his underhanded ways."[17] Nevertheless, he is able to manipulate them into letting him come into the house and visit with Tsirele. Seducing Tsirele proves to be easy. Max's sexual attraction for her is compounded by a curiosity about her world. He is a different kind of Jew. Although he thinks of religion with great intensity, ultimately he sees it as a lifestyle that one can drop at will.

Max convinces the rabbi, however, that he is willing to grow a beard and dress as an observant Jew. Perhaps the conviction of his role-play will be so strong that he actually will become a devout Jew, transcending detachment and artificiality. For Max, the rabbi and his family are a sort of Polish fresco, a set scene for which he dresses the part. Such is his ambivalence that his costume is both a disguise and a partial truth.

But how firm is Tsirele's own relationship to this apparently stable world? Singer has identified the mystery of a certain Jewish wisdom in a female character he names Shosha in the novel that bears her name.

Shosha, an undeveloped young woman, stands for a knowledge that may be confused with childishness or mental retardation. Her relationship to Jewish observance is enigmatic and unquestioned; her appearance makes her look ageless and, as a consequence, almost trans-historical. Tsirele, on the other hand, is a grown woman, and smart. In very much the same way as Max, and to his surprise, she thinks of changing her appearance.

At first, Tsirele is portrayed somewhat like Shosha in her vulnerability as "pale as if after a sickness, dressed up in a white blouse and in a light green skirt," and Max, in a fit of religiosity and melodramatic passion, thinks that he could "kiss her like a mezuzah."[18] A few pages later, however, a transformed Tsirele visits him in his hotel, markedly changed: "He looked at her, stunned. She was wearing a light-colored suit and the straw hat he had bought her. He had never seen her look so elegant. Nobody would have taken her to be the daughter of a rabbi; she could just as well be a countess. Max was suffused with joy and shame. Is it over her that I'm agonizing? I'd give my last groschen to be with her! he thought."[19]

Max's sentiment is echoed in the lyrics of many a tango: the man, hopelessly in love with a woman he deems innocent, leaves everything he has or changes his ways only to see her later and realize that she has become unworthy. Dressing in a manner that stresses one's participation in the world at large is a departure from the virtues of piety and modesty entailed by Tsirele's avowed spirituality.

Makeovers are suspect precisely because of their artificiality. In this case, what devalues Tsirele in Max's eyes is the fact that she has changed in *his* direction. She has broken with the air of holy dowdiness that surrounded her and become part of what he intended to reject.

Max expected his return home to be a rediscovery of essential roots. He hoped to be changed, made more substantial and authentic. With this character Singer provides us with an early example of what has become commonplace in American popular culture: the search for ancestral homes and learning of languages as part of a cult of connections severed by time.

Whether as pimp or observant Jew, Max attempts to shape himself as a character by including himself within a story that is already in progress; if he succeeds, he feels, fakery will turn into authenticity. Yet Tsirele's change turns everything around.

In spite of Max's free-floating energy for drama, his willingness to take any shape, like a liquid in a vessel, renders no positive results. The voyage to his place of birth is thus portrayed as the most trivial of pursuits.

Max's experiences have a certain hollowness, and even

worse, Tsirele's new manner of dressing suggests her own may be the same. The timelessness of religious ritual and culture has been cracked by a costume; Max's influence has triumphed over her upbringing. Standing before Max, Tsirele is testimony to the superficial nature of his trip. The spiritual distance between skeptical Buenos Aires and Jewish Poland has vanished. Nevertheless, Max reacts with passion to her visit, feeling that his virility has been restored.

In the end, Max goes to prison because he fires a shot as he is about to have sex with Reyzl, an unscrupulous woman who stands in opposition to whatever Tsirele may have represented. "They all stared at him in silence. Everything had been ordained from the beginning. Max was seized with a kind of piety mixed with fear. He, Max, had come to Warsaw to perpetrate all this craziness for only one purpose, to realize his dream."[20]

Finally, Max has been recognized. The cast of characters he has hoped to join has identified and defined him. Yes, he does belong among them, in Warsaw. *In prison.* He is *the* Jewish criminal, a man who twists and changes, ready for everything and, because of that, belonging nowhere but in a lock-up. Thus, a voyage to roots approaches perfection. Hollowness and frantic role-playing come to an end. With relief, Max assumes the name proposed in the novel's title: *Shoym,* Scum.

His place of birth is now devoid of the indifference to origins evoked in Lispector's "The Chicken" and "The Smallest Woman in the World." He has been discovered and defined by his motherland. The madness here is not his mother's, as in Duras's *The Lover*, and he has not even had to change languages like Sarraute.

Max has arrived home at last. These are his roots, and here he will meet his punishment. What makes the ending of Max's search so compelling is the coherence with which his life may be gauged. A truly Borgesian turn in the story has made it possible to reread a seemingly ambiguous trip as an intimate discovery of his destiny.

What would be, then, the language that is so natural to you that it will restore you to your beginnings and ease your relationship to the world? Singer in *Scum*, like Lispector, Sarraute, and Duras, tells us about attachments to a woman, be it a mother, a lover, or a bride, that fail the promise of transparency and harmony.

Did the Englishwoman kidnapped by Indians in Argentina who had almost forgotten her language in Borges's story have a child?[21] And was the broken allegiance in her voice that child's haven? Where is that place in which meanings are not compromised by misunderstandings and every voice reaches an intimate counterpart in mainstream culture?

A poetics of detachment and artificiality opens up when we face the danger of the disappearing mother, or merely the mother tongue. She leaves with a wink and the taste of blood in the mouth that Borges refers to so casually in his story. Whether to celebrate, bemoan, or be indifferent to her departure is a disquieting and insistent dilemma.

Getting a Life

Shape

Last-minute revelations or experiences have defined the way we understand lives in literature and film. The dissolute woman redeemed as she draws her last breath by an act of heroism or abnegation, the parent delivered from a life of pain by the appearance of a long-lost child, the criminal absolved by a moment of generosity, the cruel man suddenly made beautiful by a caring act that sends him to a peaceful death—all these belong in a gallery of characters that help us give shape to otherwise arbitrary facts.

Death colors everything that came before, thereby shaping life as narrative. Seemingly pointless details become meaningful as they are integrated into a context akin in its power of definition to the place of birth. Borges frequently uses death to define structure. Just like motherhood, death—at the opposite end of life—helps make sense of existence. It is the ultimate one-way ticket, both in defining an end and in grounding the array of events and experiences that lead up to it.

Revolutionaries do not want to die in bed; some people form families so as not to die alone. Bernarda Alba in Lorca's *La casa de Bernarda Alba* wants to make everybody believe that her daughter died a virgin (*mi hija ha muerto virgen*), which in her view is the greatest feminine virtue. All of these are but instances of the fear of the shapelessness imposed by everyday occurrences. Death is a fact unlike any other, with the power to sort out the banal from the relevant. Borges considered it a great privilege to reach the end knowing that death made individual experience into a necessary development imposed by destiny.

Reinaldo Arenas fled Cuba as a political and sexual refugee after being imprisoned and facing mainstream derision because of his homosexuality. His posthumous autobiography, *Antes que anochezca* (*Before Night Falls*), made into film by Julian Schnabel in 2000, is framed by two documents that shape the understanding of what he tells us about his life: an introduction that he calls "the end" in which he discloses his 1987 AIDS diagnosis and a final note to family and friends.

Terminal illness makes the body into the receptacle of a shared danger, and the person to whom it belongs into a representative of all those at risk. We are moved by the stricken and their ordeal, admire their caregivers, and participate through books, films, and television in a collective conversation about the havoc produced by various afflictions. The popularity of medical television series affirms how thoroughly we consider our physical well-being, or lack thereof, to be part of a shared storytelling.

Dying of breast cancer, childhood disease, or, until recently, AIDS, grants a particular virtue to the sick in North American culture. Physical humiliations are seen as stations of martyrdom, with the concomitant implications of endurance and selflessness.

Arenas's diagnosis, coming after frequent fevers, made him decide to leave New York for Miami, where he could die close to the sea. As it turned out, his death would not occur that way; yet he was still in charge of its scripting, as we learn from the document that closes the book, a farewell note, marked *for publication,* explaining his suicide in New York. As such, it provides an interpretation of his life, his disease, and the possible consequences of his departure.

The culprit is Fidel Castro, whose indictment makes Arenas's fate an emblem for the political and historical situation of Cuba: "The sufferings of exile, the pain of being banished from my country, the loneliness and the diseases contracted in exile would probably have never happened if I had been able to enjoy freedom in my country."[1] Castro is not only in the past; he gives sense to the future as well, and despite making the ultimate pessimistic decision to kill himself, Arenas encourages others to continue the struggle against dictatorship. Implicitly, the suicide note keeps his spirit alive by politicizing his story, placing it in a graspable collective context.

Before Night Falls begins and ends with the end. The book is a comment on its frame and, as such, sketches a clear-cut rendering of a life. Illness, exile, and Castro are the decisive organizing points. No everyday banalities, it seems to say, will impede this story, for its author is an exemplary character. Arenas's autobiography fights against the very ambiguities he so cherished for the characters in his fiction. He does not want to be like Fray Servando Teresa de Mier, the basis for arguably his best novel, *El mundo alucinante* (*Hallucinations*). When I first read the novel, I was taken with its structure and wrote an article arguing that Arenas's treatment of the multifaceted Fray Servando—part legend, part truth, incorporating the ironic storytelling mode of Borges and Cervantes—was more complex than that of historians with their naive scientism.[2] Years later, when Arenas went into exile and we were able to meet in Boston, he told me that my article had helped him become established in a world that, when he was in Cuba, seemed foreign and distant. When we talked, though, I had no idea how much his writing was about to change with his arrival in the United States.

Exile scripted a new tone for Arenas as he turned attention on himself. In contrast to the playful account of Fray Servando's exploits and the detachment from factual evidence that makes his 1967 novel *Celestino antes del alba*, based on his early years, a metaphor for the elusive possibilities of writing, he now looked for continuity and clarity.[3]

The will to shape life in *Before Night Falls* implies a flight from the sort of reading he so deftly suggested in his best fiction. If he was able to show the inadequacy of strictly historical accounts in *El mundo alucinante* and of sentimental childhood recollections in *Celestino antes del alba*, his autobiography demands a different perspective, one in which those other books become chapters to be redefined. The sense of purpose of the life chronicled in *Before Night Falls* would otherwise be too easily betrayed.

Uprootedness

Most people are not indifferent to the place where they will be buried. Many inflect their choice with symbolic value because our culture treasures continuity and believes that final resting sites indicate profound belonging. For some, too, the choice involves a summary of experience, an expression of allegiance and a recognition of roots.

Frequently, for exiles and expatriates scattered in societies that hold a loose grip on their imaginations, impending death on foreign soil is a particularly wrenching aspect of their condition. "In exile," Arenas wrote about his time in Miami, "one is nothing but a ghost, the shadow of someone who never achieves full reality. I ceased to exist when I went into exile; I started to run away from myself."[4]

There he is by the beach in a climate not so different from Cuba, living in a city resonant with Spanish and home to a rich group of Cuban émigrés, but he does not feel at home in Miami, which he describes as paranoid and gossipy. Instead, it is the streets of New York that invite Arenas. He does not seem to mind the cold, the language switch, or the sheer size of the city; it is much better than Miami, which he calls Purgatory to Havana's Hell. "[New York] took me into its fold. I felt as though I had arrived in a glorified Havana, with great sidewalks, fabulous theatres, a transportation system that worked marvelously, streets that were lively, and all kinds of people who spoke many different languages. I did not feel like a stranger in New York."[5] And so he chose to die there, in this fictionalized Havana. The mirage of the city worked for Arenas as for others before him. He had found a way to feel at home.

Perhaps the mimicking in Miami of an increasingly distant Cuban society alienated him; perhaps the cocktail parties and the surrounding chitchat were enough to make him want to leave. But in going back to New York he was also abandoning a certain sense of himself as a man associated with the sea. It was as though he had given himself a first reading as a beach-loving native of his island but suddenly realized that he was not in fact the islander he thought. The imagery of the sea, the heat, the fragrances and sensuality of unending summers all gave way to the wonder of New York, a city pulsating with different languages, where so many were foreign-born, just like Arenas himself.

His well-being in New York, however, implied a transformation of the very meaning of Havana. That name no longer signified a specific place; rather, it became a state of mind, an invitation to decode mysteries. Without being aware of it, Arenas made a transition from the Cuban exile lamenting his uprootedness to the cosmopolitan flâneur exploring myriad urban opportunities and challenges. At ease in one city because it improves the memory of the other, he takes Havana into the realm of utopia. His place is now no place. Neither the actual New York nor the actual Havana, he now inhabits the ever-shifting, subjectively mythologized crisscrossing of streets that Julio Cortázar called *la zona.*[6]

The autobiography does not render an account of the transition. We are not told how it came to be, how the city in fact seduced Arenas. Both here and in Isaac Bashevis Singer's *Shadows on the Hudson,* we have the sense that the compactness of the expatriate communities in Miami, whether Eastern European Jews or counterrevolutionary Cubans, is claustrophobic. Arenas is doubly uprooted, and perhaps on the verge of switching out from the nostalgia implied in his evocation of homeland, when he decides to take his own life. His autobiography offers the way out of its own constraints through the perception he has of New York. But it is too late to open up the frame and forge a sense of national identity that would overcome geographical distinctions.

Bodily pleasures

Sex plays an important role in *Before Night Falls.* Arenas defines himself as a seeker of sexual encounters; indeed, being successful in the hunt and arousing men are so much part of how he sees himself that he considers death preferable to going unnoticed. In the introduction, he describes being overcome by the desire to die when, already in the United States, he went into a public restroom only to find erotic activities in progress—and yet no one even acknowledged his presence. Arenas's account of his sexual activity (he claims at one point to have had some five thousand different sexual partners) is not so much praise for freedom as nostalgic recollection, a counterpoint to his physical deterioration due to his illness. He felt old and ready to end his life. By the time of his suicide at age forty-seven, the retrospective account of his life had an implied readership that clearly shared his desires or, at least, his expectations.

Cuba in his account is a very different story. He tells, for example, about an encampment where as a teenager he was locked up with over two thousand other men. "One would think, as I do now," he comments, "that this was an opportunity for me to develop my homosexual tendencies, and to have many erotic relationships. I had none." He adds: "In those days I endured all the prejudices typical of a macho society fired up by the Revolution. In that school, overflowing with virile militancy, there seemed to be no place for homosexuality."[7]

He longs for a youthful, attractive body. Its loss, simultaneous with his exile, becomes an integral part of his identity. When he left Cuba, he abandoned the place where he experienced his most intense sexual rewards. In a manner reminiscent of magical realism, he portrays himself then as being aroused by the sight of groups of men in idyllic surroundings. As a six-year-old on a walk with his grandmother at a place called Río Lirio, he sees something that becomes an unending gift: thirty men bathing in the river. "All the young men of the neighborhood were there, jumping from a rock into the water. To see all those naked bodies, all those exposed genitals, was a revelation to me: I realized without a doubt that I liked men."[8]

The rural context of these early experiences; Arenas's household with its eleven aunts; the walks in the woods, during which he on occasion encountered a fetus or a dead child; and the pervasive mention of special powers and hyperbolic situations—all these set him apart as a character.[9] Through this scene, his own body is made youthful, removed from the present.

Writing about himself as a child, Arenas points out the exotic and stresses otherness in terms current in the literature of the time. Ironically, the much-derided perspective of Gabriel García Márquez, regarded as an enemy by anti-Castro forces, colors his sexual and childhood self-portrayal. Although he resented being regarded as a curiosity in Miami, by drawing attention to his early years with their wondrous sexual opportunities and peculiar beliefs, the world he sees himself as emerging from seems designed to appeal to curiosity seekers. A contagion has taken place, and those whose gaze set him apart as foreign before have now been internalized as the eye that invents the author in his autobiography.

The evocation of the Cuba of his youth contains accounts of the household, with scenes of masturbation and images connecting him to the soil presented as instances of self-discovery and pleasure. When babies are born, the umbilical cords are rubbed with dirt; his first crib, in fact, was a hole dug in the soil. *Tierra* in Spanish may be translated into English, depending on the context, as *dirt*, *soil*, or *earth*. Although the translator has chosen *earth*, I think *dirt* or *soil* renders better the raw feeling of the original text; it is, after all, from the abject and the unclean that some of Arenas's most significant physical experiences arise.

Arenas talks about how he views the body in Cuba: "The earth was there when we were born, in our games, in our work, and, of course, at the moment of our death. The corpse, in a wooden box, would be returned directly to the earth. The coffin would soon rot and the body had the privilege of dissolving in that earth and becoming a vital, enriching part of it. The body would be reborn as a tree, as a flower, or as a plant that, one day, perhaps someone like my grandmother would smell and be able to divine its medicinal properties."[10] Earth (soil) and dirt (*tierra*, which also refers to the planet) anchor the body in the soil, and the pastoral evocation of the first consciousness of homosexual attraction while watching men bathing in the river suggests that desire is equally basic to his experience.

A Cuba more essential than political realities is presented here; its power is nature and the energy of youth. Exile is for Arenas a farewell to his healthy body and his most intense moments of sexual awareness. The highly mythologized wish for freedom that took him to Miami, the beach, and the familiar sounds of Spanish proved too literal a reading of his past. New York offered itself instead as a more accurate place for rebirth and self-memorialization.

A great man

Who was Arenas and what place did he give himself in Cuban cultural history? His sexual and political dissidence on the island, while real and punishing, allowed him to be close to Virgilio Piñera and José Lezama Lima, among the most important Cuban writers of his time. Not only did he make friends with them, but he also benefited from their counsel and mentorship.

His association with Virgilio Piñera was a key to his productivity. He first met Piñera in 1966 after he received honorable mention from UNEAC (Unión Nacional de Escritores y Artistas de Cuba) for his novel *El mundo alucinante*. Piñera gave Arenas his phone number and offered advice, after telling him that José Antonio Portuondo and Alejo Carpentier had voted against awarding him first prize. Editorial and bibliographical advice followed, together with friendship. In *Before Night Falls*, Carpentier, a representative of official Cuba and a heterosexual, is portrayed as a villain.

Arenas apparently knew from the outset that he deserved prestige and recognition. Unlike Witold Gombrowicz, whose friendship with Virgilio Piñera in Argentina became a source of wonder and gossip for Arenas, he did not want to remain on the sidelines.

Gombrowicz believed that if he was to write well, he had to preserve a certain silence around himself. Arenas, in contrast, claimed membership in a collectivity, even if that contradicted his proud self-definition as an outsider. Anxious not to appear to crave the invisibility of a Gombrowicz, he grasped every opportunity to be included in the community.

Gombrowicz took advantage of his exile to cultivate his strangeness. Free to be perceived as embodying whatever pose he took, removed from the knowing look of his countrymen, he basked in the ambiguities created by his simultaneous desire to be recognized as a great author and to disappear from national histories because of mainstream mediocrity. Arenas was no eccentric, rather the opposite, and the prestige of national literary history was something he coveted and believed he fully deserved from the very outset of his career. Because he was so sure of his value, he wrote without a single thought of the suspicion of opportunism that a critical reader might develop: "With two of my novels (although not yet published) winning awards, and thanks to the influence of my then lover Rafael Arnés, I was able to get a job at the Cuban Book Institute, directed by Armando Rodríguez."[11]

In Arenas's world, while revolutionary machismo was uniformly condemned, favoritism in a gay enclave was seen as normal, even desirable. In the same section of the autobiography he comments on the fact that the then head of the Cuban Book Institute, Armando Rodríguez, had the most handsome male lover: "His name was Héctor. He was one of those men who radiated such overwhelming beauty that it was impossible to continue writing after he had passed through the hallways. I do not know how Armando, an important official of the regime, managed to hold on to such a handsome lover without inciting the envious, who did not have access to Héctor, to disrupt the relationship or to arrange to have Armando removed from his position. But Armando was a friend of Fidel Castro's, just like Alberto Guevara, whose scandalous homosexual life was well known all over, especially in Havana." And so on and so forth. The coziness of the arrangement is offered uncritically, even though there was an ongoing persecution of homosexuals, condemning them to a furtive and dangerous existence that was eventually shared by Arenas himself.

A tale of literary associations accompanies the recollections of sex with hundreds (or thousands) of men. The resulting picture is one of clandestine encounters and a succession of love affairs counterposed to the image of an ambitious writer keen on achieving a central role in his country's literature. Through the autobiography Arenas tries to occupy the spaces available for exemplary dissidents, both political and sexual, as well as to great writers recognized by all and unjustly marginalized authors. The solidarity he feels with others is a key to understanding the various economies in which he inscribes himself.

He compares himself to José Martí, a monument of Cuban history and literature who also wrote from New York. In so doing, he dispels the idea that the writings of a Cuban in exile would be inconsequential to the life of the island. Yet he is also distressed by what he finds in Miami. Here, anxiety about his legacy is patent. While as a newcomer he finds it easy to be published, he encounters excellent Cuban writers who are living in obscurity and poverty. Although he—unlike Gombrowicz—thought there had to be a correlation between writing excellence and official recognition, he found that the lack of money and publishing opportunities for writers he truly admired to be scandalous. Nonetheless, he says, to a large extent it was the fault of Cubans themselves.

He criticizes writers both on the island and in exile for their mediocrity and for their jealousy of their more accomplished counterparts. He presents as an emblem of the fate of the Old Havana intelligentsia the cases of Lydia Cabrera, a grand dame living a bleak existence in Miami, almost blind, and Carlos Montenegro, whom Arenas regards as a great writer, surviving on welfare in an obscurity that lasted until his death. The contempt with which Arenas views the large number of Cuban poets in Miami—and the regard in which he holds the writers who enjoyed less success—places him among the highest-quality literary figures, a permanent victim of every kind of political, sexual, and literary slight, not only as an individual but as part of a group.

Arenas's autobiography is a travel document and a historical chart. We follow his life as it is torn apart by Cuban politics, both on and off the island. By implication, Arenas himself is shrouded in purity. Disease, poverty, and forced uprootedness have delivered him greatness.

Home

For Arenas, the utopia conceived of now as home, New York, has helped rewrite the past. Characters are presented in a fresco of Cuban life that arranges them in conflicting plots trying to unseat one another while engaging in associations in which abnegation, heroism, and love are still possible. In his autobiography, Arenas derides academics in the United States and Europe for their leftism and puts down politically engaged writers as paying less attention to literature than to ideological causes.

In a 1987 interview, Arenas stressed his admiration for Borges:

> Literature is something mysterious that can't be labeled and categorized as useful or not useful — literature goes beyond the political machinery. . . . Borges's greatness existed in the fact that he placed his faith in the act of creation itself, a faith that went beyond the circumstances in which he lived. . . . Poetry is the source of everything. I read poetry. That is why I have always admired Borges, who is a great poet.[12]

As for himself, it is not content but the rhythm of sentences that he wants to be recalled by, he says. Poetry is at the root of all literature. And—rather conveniently for Arenas—the two writers who best knew this, Lezama Lima and Borges, were close to his political views. Cortázar and Carpentier (both identified with Castro's regime), in contrast, he referred to with condescension. It is as if Arenas, after stating a libertarian high-risk view of literature, recoils from conflict when he establishes a genealogy for himself.

How does the autobiography measure up against his ambitious view of the role of intellectuals and the primacy of his politically disinterested idea of literature?

Another remarkable Cuban writer, Severo Sarduy, who died in Paris in 1993 and, together with Guillermo Cabrera Infante, represented to the world Cuban literature abroad, was instrumental in getting Arenas published in French.

His posthumous novel *Pájaros de la playa* is, like Arenas's autobiography, traversed by images of the ravages of AIDS.[13] To the question of whether it might be possible to inscribe one's body and one's life in a book that would still be faithful to the writer's most intense literary insights, Sarduy's text suggests an affirmative answer, while Arenas's autobiography remains an oddity among his works.

Sarduy, unafraid of misunderstandings, took esthetic and personal risks in *Pájaros*. Characters suffering from an unnamed ailment exchange disguises, nicknames, minor and major vices, as though they were in a fashion parade. They massage their bodies, take medication, and agonize in an atmosphere rich in the poetry of decadence and the stale humor of death. But this is of course no autobiography, although those readers who know the circumstances of the author's demise can glimpse a body in pain. Writing already as though death had erased his presence but not himself as a writer, Sarduy seems to wink at us in choosing a lonely and silent exit. His farewell, a subtle and elusive piece of writing, is one of the best novels he ever published.

Arenas's celebration of poetry and dismissal of the *novela de testimonio*, advocated by Miguel Barnet and the Cuban establishment, is apparent in his parody of historical sources in *El mundo alucinante*. But when telling his own story, he adhered to the norm. How could he trust that the reconstruction of his life would not be misunderstood? He did not want to be another Fray Servando Teresa de Mier, falling somewhere between legend and fact.

Would it be enough to go back to the soil and become

a flower, one with nature, as he suggests in recalling his childhood? The formidable intellectual energy he displayed even in illness speaks to his faith in literature. His autobiography brings him to life in the minds of readers as a monumentalized version of people he met, victims of sexual and political persecution. Torn between the hyperbole of magical realism and the demands of *la literatura de testimonio,* the character emerging from that soil is no longer free to dissolve in the earth and become one with nature. Instead, he wishes to control the way in which he is understood, choosing the moment of his death and erasing ambiguities in the account of his experiences. Raw, but nevertheless wanting to preserve the idea that a writer should have a place in his national literature, Arenas demands that New York *be* Havana. He has left, but he is no wanderer; his exile will not involve the choices made by Milan Kundera, who started writing in French, or Vladimir Nabokov, who gave up Russian for English. A master of excess and the baroque, he sets his own limits in death and wishes to project a story whose recipient is both here and there, in a redefinition of the national as foreign.

Foreignness and Ridicule

A teacher of foreign languages?

Foreign language and literature departments in the United States sustain dreams of alternative identities. Universities boast dormitories in which students are allowed to speak only in the target language, and techniques for teaching everyday communication suggest that there is a continuum between speaking a language and actual knowledge of what is loosely termed a foreign culture. The aim is practical: ready understanding of everyday situations and acknowledgment of allegedly essential cultural characteristics. Rather than awakening students to ideas that may be shared by others regardless of language, language instruction offers a combination of eating and greeting habits sprinkled with historical and journalistic information.

The shying away from straightforward reading and writing as a means of studying a language places foreign language classrooms in American colleges in a middle ground between focused conversation practice for travel and disinterested learning.

A quaint subculture of language teachers made up of exiles, visitors, and North Americans with the coveted native or near-native language skills populate these departments. Among them are scholars, poets, linguists, and dilettantes with expertise in opera, film, and literature. Enthusiastic and vigorous though their teaching often is, it is accompanied by the sense that students may just not be capable of grasping the true depth of what they are offered in class. A favorite poem, a quotation from a piece of fiction, or the name of an admired writer are items smuggled into language classes by teachers who wistfully decry the limitations of curricula in which viewing and discussing films and journalistic articles could very well be the most intellectually demanding items.

It is in this post-literary society that Nabokov's character Pnin appears, a recent arrival to the United States who finds himself teaching his native language, in this case Russian, to college students.

Nabokov's own relationship to the United States, where he lived and taught for many years, undoubtedly informed the sharply humorous perspective with which he portrays the disconcerted newcomer who can barely intuit the agendas of his young students. As for his own relationship to bilingualism, Nabokov decided at a certain point that he would switch languages: stop writing in Russian and devote himself wholly to doing it in English. Unlike other writers, he did not want to straddle between two languages. Pnin is also adamant about becoming integrated into North American culture. Like Nabokov, he has no investment in "Leninized

Russia" and, as he starts teaching at Waindell College, he tries to take on a new identity. Dressing the part is essential:

> Prior to the nineteen-forties, during the staid European era of his life, he had always worn long underwear, its terminals tucked into the tops of neat silk socks, which were clocked, soberly colored, and held up on his cotton-clad calves by garters. In those days, to reveal a glimpse of that white underwear by pulling up a trouser leg too high would have seemed to Pnin as indecent as showing himself to ladies minus collar and tie; . . . Nowadays, at fifty-two, he was crazy about sunbathing, wore sport-shirts and slacks, and when crossing his legs would carefully, deliberately, brazenly display a tremendous stretch of bare skin.[1]

Pnin has changed to fit his own idea of his surroundings. But appearances are deceiving. He is a disconcerted, ill-at-ease man who takes the wrong train and misses a lecture he was to deliver. As a result, there are no witnesses for his newly acquired looks. What good is style without a public? Bound nowhere and missing his appointment, Pnin is out of place despite his efforts. But he is also a learned man and a bemused observer of the United States. The Russia he left is no longer. The new persona he tries to build is thus a composite of his insights about the United States and his faithfulness to something intermittently resembling an intellectual pursuit.

For him, life at Waindell College imposes the special isolation frequently found in foreign language departments. At a certain point he has only one student, "plump and earnest Betty Bliss," in the transitional group and less than a hand-

ful at the other levels. His teaching of the Russian language
bears no relationship to that of

> those stupendous Russian ladies, scattered all over America,
> who, without having had any formal training at all, man-
> age somehow, by dint of intuition, loquacity, and a kind of
> maternal bounce, to infuse a magic knowledge of their diffi-
> cult and beautiful tongue into a group of innocent-eyed stu-
> dents in an atmosphere of Mother Volga songs, red caviar,
> and tea; nor did Pnin, as a teacher, ever presume to approach
> the lofty halls of modern scientific linguistics, that ascetic
> fraternity of phonemes, that temple wherein earnest young
> people are taught not the language itself but the method of
> teaching others to teach that method; which method, like a
> waterfall splashing from rock to rock, ceases to be a medium
> of rational navigation but perhaps in some fabulous future
> may become instrumental in evolving esoteric dialects.[2]

Renowned linguist Roman Jakobson is frequently quoted
as having said that he spoke Russian in twelve different
languages. An eloquent commentary on the all too audible
obstacles to meshing with the natives, his quip also points
to a quaint faithfulness to the homeland. By not losing
their accents, some keep their lives in their native country
through their diction, thus incorporating the resonances of
a distant place into every new verbal exchange.

· Pnin speaks English idiosyncratically. His accent and
frequently mistaken constructions clearly indicate that he is
thinking in Russian. His appearance is, like his speech, an
effort at translation. In his classes, he tries to convey who
he is in this different context by telling students how he was

admitted to the United States. Just as Witold Gombrowicz compulsively retold the account of his arrival in Argentina, Pnin needs both to justify his presence and separate himself from the randomness of his current condition by telling how he traversed the distance. The trip itself is a testimony to the fact that he existed elsewhere, in a place where he was not a rarity and he had no foreign accent.

In Pnin's day, study-abroad semesters were not as common as today. Then, the drama of geographical distance was more intense because professors were messengers from the unfamiliar. The cloak of foreignness benefited teachers such as Pnin: exoticism completed the experience of having contact with a native.

Students gave Pnin mixed reviews. Some enjoyed him, while others complained that he bootlegged poetry into classes where they were expecting only to learn the Russian language. Neither an abstractly minded linguist nor an intuitive transmitter of the customs of Russia, Pnin does not quite fit into Waindell College, and the cast of characters surrounding him makes him look even more awkward in contrast.

By introducing the student Betty Bliss into Pnin's life, Nabokov—not unlike Lispector in "The Smallest Woman in the World"—stages a cultural encounter between two figures closely linked but at the same time very separate and distinct. In the case of Little Flower and the anthropologist, the connection is puzzlingly called love; for Pnin, it is learning. The questions remain open: What do Lispector's characters have in common that would give love meaning for them as a couple? How can Pnin and his students develop a productive relationship when students, who wish simply to learn Russian, view their professor as whimsically attached to the literary qualities of the language? What is at stake here is not just a language barrier, but the kind of cultural and generational rift so ubiquitous in Nabokov's work.

In choosing to write in English, Nabokov did not abandon his eccentricity, the detachment that allowed him to observe details and gestures with minute attention. HH's fascination with Lolita is, as well, a love affair, in spite of perceptions about the energy of American youth and its vulgarity. If the passion for Lolita reads more like his descent than her victimization at the hands of a corruptor of minors, it is because the novel shows youth as having the power to erase cultural and moral considerations. It is as though the force of the future were embodied by English and by the formidable capacity of its young practitioners to draw the curtain on a certain way of understanding tradition and moral strictures.

Perhaps the ones described with least compassion in *Pnin* are the students. They are seen as well-adapted natives, pathologically wholesome and too inclined to the rural life to have any meaningful relationship to culture. The faculty includes the chairman of a language department whose ignorance of what is actually taught there enables him to be all the more competent as a leader, for he will not be distracted from his administrative duties by undue interest in academic subjects.

Nabokov's *Pnin* suggests that the teaching of a foreign

culture, even by those who are supposed to know it best, leads inevitably to ridicule. The ignorance of students and administrators on the one hand, and the misplaced earnestness of the few students who strive to excel on the other, are part of a relationship with whatever is understood as foreign in which true learning is lost, or at best, bracketed.

A circuit of lectures and foreign culture discussions is portrayed as a smorgasbord that trivializes both subject matter and participants. Beyond parodying life on an American campus, *Pnin* portrays the irreversible nature of exile. The Russia that Pnin left will never exist again, and the United States he has encountered is only a farce. In the States, he is a character, a caricature of the opportunities opened up for travel and intellectual survival.

Pnin is, as well, a novel about local color. It makes fun of national idiosyncrasies and emphasizes material details, inviting us to join in as public: let's look at how you wear your undergarments in the States versus Russia; let's appreciate the differences in food, sunbathing, and weight. Pnin may look funny, but so do his colleagues and students in the exaggeratedly clear-cut ethnic and social differences depicted by the novel.

Pnin's parody of exoticism as consumerism of the picturesque suggests that a humble but decisive form of knowledge about humanity emerges from the arbitrariness with which individuals are tossed in different directions by history. Struggling with the ignorance and youth of his students, a more mature but somewhat ridiculous Americanized Pnin is learning, like them, the lessons of displacement.

Partially understood conversations, awkward dress, and the risk of ridicule imply an audience in the world of Pnin. But what about the foreigner's invisibility to society at large? In the work of Nina Berberova, absent-minded women and an unwillingness to engage in emotional situations abound. A good part of her fiction is set in Paris, and there are striking affinities not only with the most invoked influence of her work, Gogol, but also with the detailed observation of Nathalie Sarraute. The rhythm of her writing is very different from Sarraute's, however, lacking her fast-paced chains of association. Instead, Berberova wants us to slow down and reflect, to savor the relative apathy of her characters and accompany them within that state of in-betweenness that Lispector knew so well, a place of neither action nor complete withdrawal.

Nina Berberova is frequently referred to as an American writer of Russian origin. She would have probably been surprised to be perceived as clearly anchored in any of the countries in which she spent her life. She was born in St. Petersburg in 1901 and died in 1993, having spent the last portion of her life, starting in 1958, teaching Russian at such American institutions as Yale, Middlebury College, and Princeton. Like Pnin, Berberova had no sympathy for Communist Russia and, prompted by the persecution of intellectuals, left in 1922, already a published poet. Her first stop was Berlin, a lively center for émigré Russian intellectuals and artists at the time. She moved around Europe, eventually taking up residence in Paris in 1925. She lived in Paris for two and a half decades, and the city had a strong mark on her work. It is, indeed, through translations of her books into French that she became known to a wider public. Further translations into English contributed to her becoming a celebrity in the literary world at large.

The stimulus to keep on writing in Russian came from her insertion in the Russian émigré community. Like Witold Gombrowicz, who published in Polish in *Kultura,* a magazine based in Paris, Berberova worked for several Russian publications in France.

The characters in her books are far from comfortable in their surroundings. They are haunted by a sense of the lightness of their existence and frequently appear to be on the verge of giving up on life. *The Book of Happiness,* published in English in 1996, is, among her novels, the one that renders her most intense evocation of Russian exiled life in Paris.

In the novel, a gallery of characters are brought together by the suicide of Sam Boon, a childhood friend of the protagonist, Vera. His death sets the stage for an evocation of the past as a rejoinder to suicide. Grandiose though the pretext is, the novel is written in a minor key, with intimacy always taking precedence over cultural generalization.

There are no great pronouncements of attachment to Russia, rather, a wistful recollection of details. This is not the rich cultural world implied in *Pnin.* Instead it evokes the senses, returning almost obsessively to scenes from the past. Berberova's gaze privileges the marginal, the unnoticed: the way water flows, an eyebrow is arched, food smells. Her characters live on the outskirts of Paris or in neighborhoods that resist folkloric representation. At one point in the novel, Vera takes a walk at night. As she strolls, she is able, for the first time, to uncover a layer of the city that had remained hidden to her: "She really didn't know Paris like this, nighttime Paris, all black and lit up. She walked for rather a long time, reluctant to ask directions; her instinct led her, and suddenly she came upon an intersection—almost a square it was so wide—where the soundless fountains in its four corners gushed gray."[3]

Borges once remarked that what makes the best literature of the Argentine pampas great is that it does not mention landscape or other picturesque elements. For him, the insistent presence of the vast countryside grew from implication rather than description. The same may be said about Paris in Berberova's fiction.

The peculiar emptiness of certain streets, the mix of grayness and style, of nondescript outskirts and humble apartments where space is at a premium, are interspersed with flashes of beauty that recall a rich past. Not a traveler's notes, they are inextricably woven into the characters' circumstances. Soon after seeing the city at night, Vera's thoughts travel to "fussy little details. For instance, how many people could she invite to her apartment (how many chairs and armchairs?). She would invite everyone. Who could tell her what she ought to do in these situations, how she was to act?"[4] She is not a tourist in Paris; she is settled there, and everything she sees is part of the experience of belonging, however loosely, to the place.

Professor Pnin plays with language and culture to ease communication but ends up being caught in the novel's humor, a quaint, laughable figure. But who is to exercise the right to laughter?

Cross-cultural transmission, condemned by definition to error and misdirection, celebrates its detours in the Nabokov novel as it leaves behind the illusion of univocal roots and origins. Russian recollections frozen in the past are offered to students reluctant to participate in the exchange. Students and U.S. faculty on the campus, swept by the parodical energy of the novel, are every bit as amusing and artificial as their image of foreigners.

The humor when aggressively pitched condemns the view that cultures are radically different from one another. Still, the relative universalism of Nabokov's perspective does not posit an easy relationship between different cultural realms. If we leave *Pnin* and go to *Lolita*, we realize that the full impact of insurmountable difference lies in time rather than in language. Lolita's power resides in her youth. For someone of another generation, she breathes the air of a different historical age, with its vulgarity, ignorance of literature, and lack of culture; she is the emissary of something basic, plastic, and foreign.

Loving Lolita entails a pessimistic view of a culturally impoverished present and future. Suspicion of the young pervades Nabokov's fiction and gives it its idiosyncratic aristocratic tone: there is no place to go back to, but neither is there any hope in the future.[5]

Because the world of Berberova's fiction is turned inward, the effect of estrangement is different from Nabokov's. It has more affinities with the detachment exuded by the young woman in Sarraute's *Childhood*. The streets of Paris may be familiar to her, but living in her father's apartment as an unwanted guest, a semi-intruder in the family to which she only half belongs, qualifies her as a stranger.

Like Sarraute, Berberova perceives the value of the breezy freedom with which certain characters speak in their foreign accent. As she explains of another character in *The Book of Happiness*, "For some reason, Lise liked to say 'I love you' to everyone in her poor Russian, even though she knew only a few words of the language. Once she had even said 'I love you' to Vera. She arrived for Alexander Albertovich's funeral preoccupied but elegant as ever and so cozy and soft, so silky and fragrant, bedecked in black feathers and pointy little pins, that Vera was glad to see her."[6]

Saying "I love you" or anything else with an accent, like Lise and the mother in Sarraute's *Childhood*, implies self-assurance; correct pronunciation is a mere detail. What really matters is the speaker's presence, her right to play with languages any way she wants because she is somebody who lives beyond the constricting rules of correctness.

Vera, in *The Book of Happiness*, does not have Lise's freedom. She needs Lise's efficiency, her capacity to function in the world. Berberova is fascinated by the subtleties of humiliation and dependence. Her novel *The Accompanist* perhaps demonstrates this aspect of her work most clearly, but it is only one depiction of how those perceived as losers develop dependencies on overwhelming characters, mostly stronger women described as self-assured and oblivious to their weaker counterparts. The piano accompanist in this novel is overshadowed by the beautiful and glamorous singer for whom she plays. Her servility to the singer hides a powerful resentment that ultimately delivers her back to a life of mediocrity after having tasted the pleasures of Paris.

The position of the onlooker, the one who remains invisible to most, bears a strong relationship to that of the exile, whose ties to the mainstream are less rooted in time than those of natives. Berberova focuses on the more restricted world of domesticity, delineating characters and situations to which dependence comes so naturally that it verges on arrogance.

Lise's capacity to say things with the wrong accent only enhances her self-assurance. It is a positive mark of her overpowering presence, even as it underscores Vera's responsibility for her own submissiveness. In both *The Book of Happiness* and *The Accompanist*, the subservient character digs in so deeply that she shows the one in authority to be petty and undeserving. Berberova shares with Lispector and Rhys the cult of the second fiddle. It is as though the kid in the schoolyard who is picked on has come back for another round, this time ostentatiously displaying her weakness as a source of strength. Not belonging anywhere may well be the best way to hold one's own value as an enduring but pressing secret.

Where to go?

When Vera goes for a walk at night in Paris, she has somewhere to go and ends up taking a cab to her destination.

She will be able to say *I love you* to a man and start a new life—an optimistic twist given that the novel opened up with suicide.

Around the same time, in the midst of the cultural and literary buzz of émigré Paris, other women make their way from hotel to hotel wondering where they will be in another week or two. We encounter them in tango lyrics and in the work of Jean Rhys, for whom love was, above all, a way of thinking about female displacement.

Although their years coincided, Jean Rhys and Nina Berberova created characters with very different senses of what it meant to be associated with others as friends or lovers. Berberova preserved such deep roots to her homeland that her French fictions are still, paradoxically, very Russian. Nabokov, in *Lolita* and *Pnin*, was all about the frictions between generations and, to a varying extent, about the Russian-American encounter. What makes Jean Rhys different is her double estrangement.

Jean Rhys was born in Dominica in 1890. Her mother was Creole and her father a Welsh doctor. As a white girl growing up among Afro-Caribbeans, she was already an exception. She left to go to school in England in 1907 and appears to have returned to Dominica only once, in 1936. Although she tried in some of her early works to create black voices and characters, it is in the novels and stories that take place in France, written from the point of view of a white foreign woman, that she achieved a voice that is discernibly hers. She remained haunted by Dominica, however, and nourished an admiration for the vitality of an

Afro-Caribbean community to which she would have liked to belong. Dominica appears time and again in her prose as a space of unachieved harmony, one still operative as a source of contrasts.

Good Morning Midnight, After Leaving Mr. McKenzie, Voyage in the Dark, Quartet, and the stories collected under the title *Tigers Are Better Looking* bring her most searing and subtle figurations of uprootedness. Because of their concentration and measured effect, they recall the rhythm of poetry, while *Wide Sargasso Sea,* her best-known work, is more conventional.

Like Berberova, Lispector, Duras, and Sarraute, Jean Rhys invents a low-key world rife with secrets, elusive sensations, and moments of concentration on seemingly minor details. For her characters, intimacy is the biggest challenge and the most questionable possibility. Perhaps that is why she achieves such a close relationship with an implied reader, who fills the void that separates one character from another, following them through every failed personal encounter.

With nowhere to go, strolling in Paris as a debased nonintellectual flâneur, her heroines epitomize the aimless woman, born in a land that she feels she has no right to claim as her own.

What should I wear?

The beautiful Marya Zelli opens *Quartet,* a novel believed to have been based on Jean Rhys's complicated affair with her discoverer and mentor, Ford Maddox Ford, when she gets up from her table in the Café Levenue in Montparnasse after having sat there for an hour and a half. Marya Zelli is no Pnin. As she walks, the reader knows that passersby admire her and that strangers try to talk to her in the street because of her attractiveness. She shakes them off by faking that she can't understand French. But when her shady husband is imprisoned, her good looks start working against her. She becomes self-conscious and fears being found out as a poseur.

Marya Zelli becomes destitute, and the relationships she establishes with others are now designed to get food and a roof over her head. She is twenty-eight years old. When she is obliged to sell her wardrobe to survive, the searching look of Madame Hautchamp, the buyer, does more than just examine her clothes. Hoping to bring down the price, the woman dismisses their usefulness; her gesture isolates Marya's pose, making it visible to the reader:

> "My sister-in-law is a *teinturiere* and I can make an arrange-
> ment with her to hang them for sale in her window, other-
> wise I could not buy them at all. As it is, I can't offer you
> much. This, for instance, this robe de soirée . . ." She
> pointed out the gem of the collection: "Who would buy
> it? Nobody. Except a woman *qui fait la noce*. Fortunately, my
> sister-in-law has several clients *qui font la noce*." "But I don't
> see why it must be that sort of woman," argued Marya. "It
> is not a practical dress," said Madame Hautchamp calmly;
> "it's a fantasy, one may say. Therefore, if it is bought at all,
> it will be bought by that kind of woman."[7]

These are not clothes for everyday people, the shabby or merely respectable who push baby carriages in Luxembourg

Garden. They are clothes for special occasions and a special kind of woman. Who is she?

Toward the end of *Quartet,* Marya is visited by a Miss Nicolson. "Miss Nicolson stood sturdily in the sun, long bodied, short legged, neat, full of common sense, grit, pop and all the rest . . . ; she wore a green scarf and a becoming hat. Her small feet were shod with crocodile-skin shoes. It was oddly shocking to catch glimpses of very hairy legs through thin silk stockings."[8] And this is the same woman who has told Marya that she loves beauty. The hairy legs and the love of beauty are accompanied by a statement about how much Miss Nicolson hates women, but Marya shrugs it off; their relationship is brief and accomplishes little. They take leave of one another, two figures striking different poses, their clothes codifying messages neatly tucked away from uncertainty.

The implication is that women may be separated into distinct groups according to how they dress. After selling her clothes, Marya becomes available to whoever might pay for new ones. She does more than shop when she chooses a hat, a dress. She is renewing her pact with life because she wants to go back into the world looking presentable.

What might it mean to look presentable when respectability is not at stake? It means existing in the present. Sporting new clothes voids her past, makes her believe that she can start all over again. But the illusion of movement, the break represented by doing away with her previous appearance, hides the more solid and choking bond that makes owning the clothes possible in the first place. It is the political relationships between the women protagonists in Jean Rhys's various fictions, be they Marya, Julia, Sasha, or whoever provides the funds for acquiring a wardrobe, that constitute the true drama. As bills pass hands we perceive the desperation entailed in the question about what to wear, for it stands for the fear of being left alone and empty, the fear of not having a *what* but a *who* to wear, and being nobody. Their affairs dissolved in failure, the sign of success for these characters is clothes to start a new story. As the narratives unravel, they become testimonies to the tenacity with which Jean Rhys's protagonists cling to their own helplessness.

Uncovering true selves

When Marya observes Miss Nicolson, she notes the hairs showing through the silk stockings as though she were a witness to some hidden identity. The unkempt legs of the woman in proper dress create a dissonance with her otherwise controlled appearance. Miss Nicolson is a mystery; she is also a lady, an established woman. As readers of Jean Rhys, we do not know how or why ladies acquire the clothes they do, but harmony between a lady and her attire is an underlying assumption. Expensive materials and muted colors exude a certain calm. No flashiness here, no nervousness about how to acquire the next outfit.

In *Voyage in the Dark*, eighteen-year-old Anna Morgan sits at a table with Laurie, described as a friend and a tart, and two casual male acquaintances, Joe and Carl. Anna is wearing one of Laurie's dresses, since the one she wanted to wear, her own black velvet, is torn. As they talk, they realize that that they are being watched from another table:

> "What do you think about the lady at the next table? She certainly doesn't look as if she loved us," I said, "I think she is terrifying," and they all laughed. But I was thinking that it was terrifying—the way they look at you. So that you know that they would see you burnt alive without turning their heads away; so that you know in yourself that they would watch you burning alive without even blinking once. Their glassy eyes that don't admit anything as definite as hate. Only just that underground hope that you'll be burnt alive, tortured, where they can have a peep. And slowly, slowly, you feel the hate back.[9]

More seasoned than Anna, Laurie fights the stare by uttering contemptuous remarks about the woman's looks: "'What right has a woman with a face like a hen's—and like a hen's behind too—to look at me like that?' Joe started to laugh. He said, 'Oh, women. How you love each other, don't you?'"[10]

This situation—a class conflict between women over dress, where the "lady side" exercises the powerful weapon of the stare to freeze the other side into reactive hostility— is a common one in Jean Rhys's work. In this passage, the man's comment frames the conflict in a larger context. For him, the woman who stares and the ones who are offended by the stare are identical.

Joe can shrug it all off as a confirmation of women's inability to love one another. As the woman at the next

table tries to humiliate Laurie and Anna with her stare, all
three become the victims of a joke between the two men.

What right has a woman who looks like a hen to cast
hostile looks at another woman? The implication is that if
the woman were in fact different from the other two, she
would be entitled to stare them down. But what would she
have to be like? To start with, she should not look like a
hen; that is, she should be attractive.

A woman can look critically at another only if she herself
has passed a test of beauty. Anna and Laurie consider the
stare a formidable aggression because it comes from an ugly
face. They cannot understand the power behind the criticism, for in their world, beauty is all that counts.

The female critical eye stems from a different domain of
experience, the pure detachment of somebody who, feeling
something beyond hate, would like to obliterate the two
other women completely, see them burn slowly in front of
her eyes. The violence of this silent combat is framed by
Joe's easygoing insult. He can use a cliché to express his
thoughts about the situation because his perception is clear:
it's just women hating other women. He is delighted by
the rediscovery of an old truth, and his laughter celebrates
his sense of women being confirmed. He can afford to be
lighthearted; the women remain blind to the violence of
his put-down because they are still choking at the hostility
evoked by the stare. Joe is comfortable in the world, as his
language shows. For him, all these women are marginal and
interchangeable.

Anna is inexperienced. Going out with Laurie and the

two men is a rehearsal for a future part. She is trying out for a role, but she is not doing very well. Her problem is she has nothing to wear, and even though Laurie lends her a dress and the use of her bathroom, the results are not altogether successful. When Laurie asks Carl what he thinks of Anna, he says: "'I don't like the way English girls dress. . . . American girls dress differently. I like their way of dressing better.' ''Ere, 'ere,' Laurie said, 'that'll do. Besides, she's got one of my dresses, if you want to know.' 'Ah,' Carl said, 'that's another story then.' 'Don't you like the dress? Carl, what's wrong with it?' 'Oh, I don't know,' Carl said. 'Anyway, it doesn't matter that much.'"[11]

The men may criticize the dress without being blamed for cruelty or detachment. Anna's sense of well-being depends so much on their approval that the reader feels relieved when Laurie avows that Anna can't help her lack of success; the dress does not, in fact, belong to her. The scene is played out in a very low key. While the criticism of the female stare from the other table conveys brutality, Carl's comment only obliquely refers to Anna. Rather, it is directed against all English girls and is to the benefit of all American girls, just as the conflict with the woman at the next table is supposed to embody a universal conflict among females. Girls, women . . . Carl talks and generalizes without considering the basis for his assertion. Through him, reality itself seems to be speaking. Laurie and Anna, the men's guests at the restaurant, have accepted their invitation and listen to their clichés. They are not angry with them, despite what they say; instead they single out the woman at

the next table because she has usurped a power of humiliation that is the male province.

The part that Anna is trying for is Laurie's life. *Voyage
in the Dark* documents the difficulty of such a passage in
almost anonymous terms. Anna's past has no weight for
her; there are a few memories, mostly of landscapes and
reluctant relatives who are happy when she leaves. She has a
neutral reaction to Laurie, a bit of revulsion at the pitch of
her voice when she drinks too much. No strong attachment
to a man counteracts the shape of Anna's relationship to
the world.

In Laurie's own terms, Anna's inexperience makes her
voyage into womanhood dark, as though she were an apathetic version of the prostitutes and lost women mentioned
by tango in the Paris of the time. In this case, though,
neither of these friends feels any passion that would distinguish them from other women of their class. They appear
to be as unsubstantial to themselves as they are to those
who, when speaking about them in their own presence, refer
to women in generalizations.

Anna's journey ends with an abortion, and even here the
doctor refuses to grant her story any individuality: "He
moved about the room briskly, like a machine that was
working smoothly. He said 'You girls are too naïve to live,
aren't you?' Laurie laughed. I listened to them both laugh-
ing and their voices going up and down. 'She'll be all right,'
he said. 'Ready to start all over again in no time, I've no
doubt.'"[12]

Like Carl and Joe, the physician feels the pleasure of repetition. Anna will be able to start all over again in no time. Although he does not know her, he knows *who* she is and understands her future so well that his recognition of her type makes Laurie laugh. He says *you girls* the way Joe said *you women,* and Laurie joins him in the hilarity. The joke is also on her, but she is a good sport and hopes that, in the end, money will come her way from male pockets to pay for her laughter.

Rights and wrongs

Pnin attempts a makeover so that he might look as though he belongs on a North American campus; Berberova's characters, though settled in Paris, stay close to their homeland through their accents and friends. Jean Rhys's women are permanently inventing themselves as French *petites femmes,* checking their makeup in purse mirrors as if they were guests and should look the part. How many chairs in the room, how to wear one's socks, where to buy and how to afford the wardrobe and the makeup are some of the questions posed by exiles who, with various levels of success, attempt to naturalize style into nationality.

Like Little Flower, however, they appear fated to remain different. There are few rights and wrongs in their appearances because their lives remain decontextualized—though this does not mean they have no anxiety about the kind of character they should become, what they should look like. Berberova could have very well remained an obscure language teacher had she not been recognized as a writer thanks to the translations of her work. She would have been just another instructor on a foreign language and literature faculty with a story and a homeland present only to herself, a less flamboyant Pnin.

The dedication to visual representations, the almost photographic eye of these authors, is a way of assimilating the foreignizing gaze as a way of writing. Paris and the United States are viewed with the same detachment that their natives feel about newcomers. Russia and Dominica, their birthplaces, remain a source for contrasts, something to help them hold back while fully knowing that there is no real return.

We Are Everywhere

Spanish-speaking children flood the schools faster than the United States can figure out what to do: Educate them in English? Make all schools bilingual to meet the literacy demands of a changing country? Women in headscarves in Europe cause people to consider the contradictions between Western social progress and the value of foreign traditions. Should there be limits to religious freedom? The once elegant Calle Florida in Buenos Aires is now overrun with Bolivians and Peruvians selling their wares. Should the invasion of the open Indian marketplace in a city that used to be so European be stopped?

People coming and going in bustling cities threaten local customs and carry their own burden of nostalgia, moments frozen in time elsewhere, in other languages and frequently with a recollection of having been of a different social class. When new populations enter a place, everyone changes, and even those who have never left their neighborhood may view the time before there were strangers there as though it belonged to a different country. They, too, suffer from the contagious effect of distance. A croissant does not taste the same when baklavas are sold in the same bakery. And what about the hand-embroidered Indian skirt topped by a mass produced T-shirt from the Gap?

Replicas can be built—Disneyland on the outskirts of Paris, Paris in Las Vegas, Madrid or London in Buenos Aires or New York, everybody's idea of the world's downtown.

Reading between the lines of the authors whose lives and works I have considered here, I recognized the meaning of an English idiom that took me a while to understand. As a young student of the language in Argentina, I was taken with the impossibility of translating *ill at ease* into Spanish. There is no literal Spanish phrase that can convey the associations of *ill* as they are perceived in combination with *ease* in a foreigner's ear.

Being ridiculed, left alone, ignored by one's own mother, a stranger to one's class, embarrassed to write when one is a writer, tempted by the voluptuousness of taking one's own life as the definitive end to partial departures—these are some of the alternatives opened up to holders of one-way tickets. Once we arrive, though, nothing remains untouched and even those who stay home are overwhelmed by the strangeness of their familiar world. They are, we are, I now know, ill at ease.

Notes

A Samovar's Tale

1. Cortázar's novel suggests two readings: one is linear, while the second skips from chapter to chapter in an order given at the start. The two-part division—"Del lado de aquí" (From here) and "Del lado de allá" (From there)—alludes to Argentina and France. One of the epigraphs of the novel is by Jacques Vaché, who is quoted in a letter to André Breton saying that nothing can annihilate a man more surely than the obligation of representing a country *(Rien ne vous tue un homme comme d'etre obligé de représenter un pays)* (Julio Cortázar, *Hopscotch,* trans. Gregory Rabassa [New York: Random House, 1967], 11).

Stranded

1. Stacy Schiff, *Saint-Exupéry: A Biography* (New York: Knopf, 1994),168.

2. *Milonguera* is derived from *milonga,* which refers both to a fast-paced, sensual dance that forms part of the tango tradition and, more generally, to a tango place or group of tango danc-ers. Tango lyrics of the early twentieth century were frequently written in *lunfardo,* an argot developed in prisons and brothels. In spite of its origins in the world of thieves and the sexual trade, lunfardo continues to be a language of communication

in Buenos Aires, though in a diluted form. Words such as *milonguera* have been incorporated into regular conversation.

3. Diana McLellan, *The Girls* (Los Angeles: LA Weekly Books, 2000), 185.

4. Annette Tappert, *The Power of Glamour* (New York: Crown Books, 1998), 169.

5. The Museo Evita in Buenos Aires offers the possibility of seeing some of her outfits, newsreels of her time, and photographic materials. There is a vast bibliography on Eva Perón and her legacy. To understand how her image was constructed over time, see María Seoane and Victor Santa María, *Esa mujer* (Buenos Aires: Cartas y Caretas, 2000).

6. Albert Londres, *Le chemin de Buenos Aires* (Paris: Albin Michel, 1927), 146–57. The intricacies of the personal relationships among prostitutes and between prostitutes and their pimps as they refer to the white slave trade from Poland and Russia have elicited great interest. Recent fictional narratives exploring the subject are Edgardo Cozarinsky's *El rufián moldavo* (Buenos Aires: Emecé, 2004) and *La polaca* by Myrtha Schalom (Buenos Aires: Ed. Norma, 2003).

How Foreign Can One Remain?

1. The first edition of Rita Gombrowicz's well-documented book *Gombrowicz en Argentine: Témoignages et documents, 1939–1963* (Paris: Denoël, 1984) contains a preface by Constantin Jelenski that speaks of the hardships Gombrowicz suffered in Argentina. The more recent edition (Paris: Denoël, 2004) includes previously unpublished documents, notably correspondence with Martin Buber, that add to the dimension of Gombrowicz's intellect. In preparing this chapter, I met with some of Gombrowicz's former associates as well as with Rita Gombrowicz.

2. Gombrowicz kept a diary during his stay (published in English in three volumes: *Diary*, trans. Lillian Vallee [Evanston, Ill.: Northwestern University Press, 1988, 1989, 1993), and it is a good source of information about his impressions both of Argentina and Europe but above all of his own positions in those societies.

3. Gombrowicz, who was thirty-five when he arrived in Argentina, made fun of his own problems with Spanish, which he learned while there. In letters to Juan Carlos Gómez (*Cartas a un amigo argentino* [Buenos Aires: Emecé, 1999]), he displays his sense of humor on the subject, imitating his own pronunciation of Spanish and exaggerating the accent of his porteño friends.

4. In time, Borges would deny that he had been well placed in Florida and reject the very idea of the alleged differences between the two groups.

5. The novel was reissued in 1982 by Centro Editor de América Latina, Buenos Aires.

6. We get a glimpse of Gombrowicz's childhood home and social background in his *Polish Memories* (New Haven: Yale University Press, 2004). There, in discussing how a bent toward snobbery was an early component of his personality, he asks himself, "How can this foolish snobbery be reconciled with my other qualities, which had made me a shrewd and critical boy with a strong sense of the comic?" (23).

7. Milan Kundera says that *Ferdydurke* deserved the place accorded to Sartre's *La nausée*, published one year later in 1938: "*Ferdydurke* a été édité en 1937, un an avant *La Nausée*, mais, Gombrowicz inconnu, Sartre célèbre, *La Nausée* a pour ainsi dire confisqué, dans l'histoire du roman, la place due à Gombrowicz" (Milan Kundera, *Les testaments trahis* [Paris: Gallimard, 1993], 293).

8. See Rita Gombrowicz, *Gombrowicz en Argentine (1939–1963)*

(Paris: Denoël, 1984). The testimonies capture the subtle put-downs of foreigners seen as not belonging to a cosmopolitan literary elite. The definition of those with a right to be part of the elite according to *Sur* is nowhere more contradictory than in the case of Pierre Drieu la Rochelle, an avowed supporter of Germany in the Second World War who enjoyed nevertheless a long relationship with Victoria Ocampo and was otherwise respected by the intensely anti-Nazi *Sur*. His correspondence with Ocampo renders a picture of their love affair and its deterioration, as well as Ocampo's leaning toward a notion of an aristocracy beyond ideological differences (*Pierre Drieu la Rochelle/ Victoria Ocampo, Lettres d'un amour défunt. Correspondance 1929–1944*, ed. Julien Hervier [Paris: Bartillat/Editorial Sur, 2009]).14. For a study of the critique of the self and the connections between Macedonio Fernández and Borges, see Alicia Borinsky, *Theoretical Fables* (Philadelphia: University of Pennsylvania Press, 1993).

9. Jacques Derrida, *La carte postale: De Socrate à Freud et au-delà* (Paris: Flammarion, 1980), xx–xx.

10. Discépolo's tangos are regularly quoted by *porteños* to interpret daily situations. Both in the mainstream and in the intellectual milieu, his lyrics spanned the gap between popular and "high" culture long before it was fashionable.

11. Witold Gombrowicz, *Trans-Atlanyik*, trans. Carolyn French and Nina Karsov (New Haven: Yale University Press, 1994).

12. In her preface to the English edition of the novel, Susan Sontag says that "Gombrowicz capers and thunders, hectors and mocks, but he is also entirely serious about his project of transvaluation, his critique of high 'ideals.' *Ferdydurke* is one of the few novels I know that could be called Nietzschean" (in

Witold Gombrowicz, *Ferdydurke* [New Haven: Yale University Press, 2000], x).

13. Gombrowicz, *Diary*, 2:180–81.

14. Ibid., 67.

15. Gombrowicz, *Trans-Atlantyk*, 3.

16. Ibid., 36.

17. Ibid., 116.

18. Gombrowicz, *Diary*, 2:46.

19. Witold Gombrowicz, *Peregrinations Argentines* (Paris: C. Bourgeois, 1994), 83–84 (my translation).

The Self and Its Impossible Landscapes

1. An interesting portrait of Pizarnik's friendships emerges in her correspondence. See Ivonne Bordelois, ed., *Correspondencia, Alejandra Pizarnik* (Buenos Aires: Seix Barral, 1998).

2. Works by Alejandra Pizarnik: *La tierra más ajena* (Buenos Aires: Botella al Mar, 1955); *La última inocencia* (Buenos Aires: Ediciones Poesía, 1956); *Las aventuras perdidas* (Buenos Aires: Altamar, 1958); *Árbol de Diana* (Buenos Aires: Sur, 1962); *Extracción de la piedra de la locura* (Buenos Aires: Sudamericana, 1968); *Nombres y figuras* (Barcelona: La Esquina, 1969); *La condesa sangrienta* (Buenos Aires: Acuarius, 1971); *El infierno musical* (Buenos Aires: Siglo XXI, 1971); *Los pequeños cantos* (Caracas: Árbol de Fuego, 1971); *El deseo de la palabra* (Barcelona: Ocnos, 1975); *Poemas* (Buenos Aires: Centro Editor de América Latina, 1982); *Textos de sombra y últimos poemas* (Buenos Aires: Sudamericana, 1982); *Obras completas* (Buenos Aires: Corregidor, 1990; new corrected edition, 1994).

3. Unless otherwise noted, all quoted passages in this section are from *Alejandra Pizarnik: A Profile*, ed. Frank Graziano, trans. María Rosa Fort, Frank Graziano, and Suzanne Jill Levine (Durango, Colo.: Longbridge-Rhodes, 1987).

Who Will Speak the Truth?

1. "The Captive," trans. Mildred Boyer, in Jorge Luis Borges, *A Personal Anthology*, ed. Anthony Kerrigan (New York: Grove Atlantic, 1961), 175.

2. "The Sham," in Jorge Luis Borges, *Dreamtigers*, trans. Mildred Boyer and Harold Borland (Austin: University of Texas Press, 1985), 31.

3. Ibid.

4. "El Zahir," trans. Dudley Fitts, in Jorge Luis Borges, *Labyrinths: Selected Stories and Other Writings* (New York: New Directions Books, 1964), 156–57.

5. Ibid., 158.

6. Ibid.

7. Ibid., 164.

8. "The Aleph," trans. Norman Thomas di Giovanni, in Borges, *Personal Anthology*, 138–39.

9. Ibid., 138.

10. "Deutsches Requiem," trans. Julian Palley, in Borges, *Labyrinths*, 142–43.

11. Ibid., 146–47.

12. "The Secret Miracle," trans. Harriet de Onís, in Borges, *Labyrinths*, 90–91.

Instructions for Taking a Leap

1. Cortázar, *Hopscotch*, 375.

2. Ibid., 319.

3. Spanish phrase: ibid., chapter 38, p. 264; English translation: p. 194.

4. Ibid., chapter 90, p. 341.

Everybody's Other World

1. Isaac Bashevis Singer, *Shadows on the Hudson*, trans. Joseph Sherman (New York: Farrar, Straus & Giroux, 1998), 13.

2. Ibid., 136.

3. Ibid., 252.

4. Ibid., 342.

5. Ibid., 343.

6. Ibid., 292.

7. Isaac Bashevis Singer, *The Certificate*, trans. Leonard Wolf (New York: Penguin, 1993); published in Yiddish in 1967.

8. Isaac Bashevis Singer, *Scum*, trans. Rosaline Dukalsky (New York: Penguin, 1992); *Shosha*, trans. Joseph Singer, Alma Singer, and Dvorah Menashe (New York: Farrar, Straus & Giroux, 1978).

9. Isaac Bashevis Singer, *Meshugah* trans. by the author and Nili Wachtel, (New York: Penguin, 1995).

10. Singer, *Shadows on the Hudson*, 73–74.

11. Junot Díaz, *The Brief Wondrous Life of Oscar Wao* (New York: Riverhead Books, 2007).

12. Oscar Hijuelos, *The Mambo Kings Play Songs of Love* (New York: Farrar, Straus & Giroux, 1989), 3.

13. Ibid., 212, 312.

14. Cristina García, *Dreaming in Cuban* (New York: Alfred A. Knopf, 1992), 134–35.

15. Ibid., 73.

16. Cabrera Infante, "La última traición de Manuel Puig," *El País*, 24 July 1990, 22–23.

Who Is the Woman of the Mother Tongue?

1. Lispector insisted that she was Brazilian and would get upset at being seen as foreign. According to her biographer Benjamin Moser, her raspy *r*'s and a lisp gave her an odd accent, which she denied was the result of having been born elsewhere (Moser, *Why This World: A Biography of Clarice Lispector* [New York: Oxford University Press, 2009], 8–9).

2. "The Smallest Woman in the World," in Clarice

Lispector, *Family Ties*, trans. Giovanni Pontiero (Austin: University of Texas Press, 1972), 95.

3. Manuel Puig's *Kiss of the Spider Woman* offers an important view of the political implications of such changes. The two protagonists of the novel are in a jail cell in a relationship precipitated by the police to make one (a leftist guerrilla) give secret information to the other (a homosexual accused of corruption of minors). In the course of their incarceration, the retelling of movie plots becomes a source of intimacy for them. The tendentious separation between love and politics permeates the most explicit layer of the novel, suggesting that radical change in one member of the couple signals unconditional love for the other, while the ending of the novel restores and emphasizes the prevalence of the political domain. For more on this, see my *Theoretical Fables: The Pedagogical Dream in Contemporary Latin American Fiction* (Philadelphia: University of Pennsylvania Press, 1993), chap. 6.

4. Lispector, *Family Ties*, 95.

5. Throughout her fiction, Clarice Lispector is eloquent about women and old age, emphasizing the idea that older women possess a special (positive) kind of intuition. Her treatment of this subject is in marked contrast to that of other twentieth-century Latin American authors (e.g., José Donoso in *The Obscene Bird of Night* and Carlos Fuentes in *Aura*), who tend to conjure up the negative traits of witches, a common trope in Hispanic letters.

6. "The Chicken," in Lispector, *Family Ties*, 51, 52.

7. In Lispector's treatment this is not uncommon. As in María Luisa Bombal's fiction, we encounter the idea that men and women speak different languages. Thus, "Little Flower" is a hyperbole of what we find elsewhere in Lispector's oeuvre.

8. Gombrowicz, *Diary*, 2:34–35.

9. In a last interview before her death in Rio de Janeiro in

1977, Lispector talked about what she saw as two extremes of her own personality—shy and daring at once—in relation to her work. See "O testamento de Clarice Lispector," *Shalom*, no. 296 (1977): 62–65.

10. Marguerite Duras, *The Lover*, trans. Barbara Bray (New York: Pantheon Books, 1985).

11. Ibid., 30.

12. Nathalie Sarraute, *Childhood*, trans. Barbara Wright (New York: George Braziller, 1984), 19.

13. Ibid., 202.

14. Max's intensely amoral behavior, combined with his sexual inadequacy and will to humiliate himself, recalls the Argentine writer Roberto Arlt's Erdosain in *Los siete locos* and *Los lanzallamas* and Balder in *El amor brujo*.

15. Singer, *Scum*, 21.

16. In the early 1900s, Polish and French women, seduced by Argentines who promised them marriage, were brought into the country and forced to become prostitutes, being unable to return to their countries due to the great cost of the trip. Their fate is recorded in novels, films, and tango. The tango "Madame Yvonne" is one of most enduring examples of the genre.

17. Singer, *Scum*, 72.

18. Ibid., 100, 101.

19. Ibid., 107.

20. Ibid., 218.

21. "Story of the Warrior and the Captive," in Borges, *Labyrinths*, 127–31.

Getting a Life

1. Reinaldo Arenas, *Before Night Falls*, trans. Dolores M. Koch (New York: Vintage, 1993), 317.

2. Alicia Borinsky, "Rewriting and Writing: Menard, Fray Servando Teresa de Mier, Borges, Arenas," *Diacritics* (Winter 1974): 20–28.

3. *Celestino antes del alba* was republished in 1982 as *Cantando en el pozo*, and in 1987 it was translated into English by Andrew Hurley as *Singing from the Well* (New York: Penguin).

4. Arenas, *Before Night Falls*, 293.

5. Ibid.

6. Julio Cortázar, *62: Modelo para armar* (Buenos Aires: Sudamericana, 1968).

7. Arenas, *Before Night Falls*, 48.

8. Ibid., 8.

9. Arenas builds his identity here in a manner reminiscent of fairy tales and Latin American exoticism. Writing about himself from the United States, he seems to adopt the gaze of a traveler willing to encounter radical difference in the new territory. In this case, the new territory is his own Cuban childhood.

10. Arenas, *Before Night Falls*, 27–28.

11. Ibid., 77.

12. Interview is reprinted in Francisco Soto, *The Pentagonía* (Gainesville: University Press of Florida, 1994), 153–54.

13. Severo Sarduy, *Pájaros de la playa* (Barcelona: Tusquets, 1993).

Foreignness and Ridicule

1. Vladimir Nabokov, *Pnin* (New York, Avon Books, 1953), 8.

2. Ibid., 10.

3. Nina Berberova, *The Book of Happiness*, trans. Marian Schwartz (New York: New Directions, 1999), 167. Berberova was particularly perceptive regarding women's sensibilities. Her biography *Moura* (New York: New York Review of Books, 2005)

reveals much about both her subject, Moura Budberg, and her perceptions about her own life.

4. Berberova, *Book of Happiness*, 167.

5. Nabokov's *Lolita* is a portrayal of the helplessness of an older man as he succumbs to difference in age. Nabokov's point of view regarding culture clash is bracketed by the current sensibility toward the rights of children vis-à-vis exploitation by adults. In *American Eve* (New York: Riverhead Books, 2008), the biography of Evelyn Nesbit, a sixteen-year-old who at the start of the twentieth century became the motive for the murder of her seducer Sanford White, Paula Uruburu studies the glamorization of youth. Nabokov's enduring fascination with the display of young women's sexuality is again present in *The Original of Laura* (New York: Knopf, 2009), an unfinished novel in which the narrator may be embodied by a voyeur who falls out of a tree while spying on the "giggles and cries of surprise" with which "the girls" talk about their companions (83).

6. Berberova, *Book of Happiness*, 143.

7. Jean Rhys, *Quartet* (New York: Harper & Row, 1990), 36.

8. Ibid., 158.

9. Jean Rhys, *Voyage in the Dark* (New York: Norton, 1982), 120.

10. Ibid., 118.

11. Ibid., 118–19.

12. Ibid., 187.

Index

Alicia Borinsky is a fiction writer, poet, and literary critic who has published extensively in English and Spanish in the United States, Latin America, and Europe. Her most recent books are *Low Blows / Golpes bajos* and *Frivolous Women and Other Sinners / Frívolas y pecadoras*, both published bilingually. She is the recipient of several awards, including the Latino Literature Prize for Fiction and a John Simon Guggenheim Memorial Foundation fellowship. She is a professor of Latin American and comparative literature at Boston University.